Based on a survey of Christian entre
book for those who feel called by Gc
those already on the journey.
Justin Welby, Archbishop of Canterbury

In today's world there are many voices seeking our attention. More
often than not they strike a discordant note. In this interesting book
we hear the words of Christians who are entrepreneurs and discover
that there is no inherent contradiction there. We also learn that the
Bible has a strong entrepreneurial theme throughout. The authors
make a good case for their conclusion that entrepreneurs have the
potential to play a major role in the church's mission. Turning
that potential into reality is essentially an entrepreneurial challenge
and is why the voice of the Christian entrepreneur is one that must
be heard.
Bill Bolton, co-author of Entrepreneurs: Talent, Temperament,
Technique

Practical, biblical, informative . . . this book conveys vividly the
voices of Christian entrepreneurs and deserves to be read by anyone
in business or training for business.
Lord Griffiths of Fforestfach, board member, Goldman Sachs International

This book is a treasure. Entrepreneurs are a fascinating group
of people, and here are the collective insights of fifty of them.
Specifically, the book examines the stories of entrepreneurs who are
fuelled by their Christian faith, and explores the role of values in the
setting up and sustaining of their businesses. From car dealerships
to toy stores, the book visits five particular entrepreneurs at work,
and reveals their leadership lessons for us all.
Eve Poole, Associate, Ashridge Business School

I loved this book. It races through the history and theology of
the Christian entrepreneurial tradition. It fills a critical gap. So
many Christians think that business is grubby and unworthy. This
book, packed with real examples and a substantial current survey
of entrepreneurs, challenges this false perception. It makes two
points convincingly. Business leaders should be proud of serving
society through offering valued goods and services for sale, while

behaving as model employers; Christian leaders should be proud
of the faith-basis that underpins their motivation. In addition, they
should be able to articulate this, clearly, modestly and confidently.
This book helps them to do so. I hope it will be widely read.
*Christopher Stephens, former Group HR Director, Exel, now DHL;
Chairman of Traidcraft, 2005–11*

This book has truth with flesh on. These stories of Christian
entrepreneurs recount their struggles, joys and successes (and some
failures) but, more importantly, they give us a window into the souls
of these men and women. Higginson and Robertshaw have crafted
a living document of fifty entrepreneurs who have made a difference
in the world, have embodied Christian values in their enterprise,
have put in a good word for Jesus when they were able, and have
used their profits as stewards – all for the sake of the kingdom of
God. This book is a delicious mixture of story and biblical reflection,
placing the challenge of starting and developing a business or
enterprise in the context of God's wonderful empowering purpose
for his much loved creatures whom he calls to 'fill the earth'. A truly
inspiring read.
*Dr R. Paul Stevens, Professor Emeritus, Marketplace Theology, Regent
College, and Chairman, Institute for Marketplace Transformation*

Like the entrepreneurs whose inspirational stories this book tells,
A Voice to Be Heard is a timely gift to the church. Richard and Kina
have produced a well-researched and highly readable book that is
biblically grounded, theologically rigorous and refreshingly original.
This excellent contribution to the growing literature on Christian
entrepreneurs will inform and inspire readers and challenge church
leaders to include entrepreneurs in their thinking and planning
around mission. I commend *A Voice to Be Heard* in the highest
possible terms.
Michael Volland, Principal of Ridley Hall and author of The Minister
as Entrepreneur

A
VOICE
TO BE
HEARD

Christian entrepreneurs
living out their faith

Richard Higginson and Kina Robertshaw

INTER-VARSITY PRESS
36 Causton Street, London SW1P 4ST, England
Email: ivp@ivpbooks.com
Website: www.ivpbooks.com

© Richard Higginson and Kina Robertshaw 2017

Richard Higginson and Kina Robertshaw have asserted their right under the Copyright, Designs and Patents Act 1988 to be identified as Authors of this work.

All rights reserved. No part of this publication may be reproduced, stored in a retrieval system, or transmitted, in any form or by any means, electronic, mechanical, photocopying, recording or otherwise, without the prior permission of the publisher or the Copyright Licensing Agency.

Unless otherwise stated, Scripture quotations are taken from the New Revised Standard Version of the Bible, Anglicized edition, copyright © 1989, 1995 by the Division of Christian Education of the National Council of the Churches of Christ in the USA. Used by permission. All rights reserved.

The extracts marked AV are from the Authorized Version of the Bible (The King James Bible), the rights in which are vested in the Crown, and are reproduced by permission of the Crown's Patentee, Cambridge University Press.

Scripture quotations marked NIV are taken from the Holy Bible, New International Version (Anglicized edition). Copyright © 1979, 1984, 2011 by Biblica (formerly International Bible Society). Used by permission of Hodder & Stoughton Publishers, an Hachette UK company. All rights reserved. 'NIV' is a registered trademark of Biblica (formerly International Bible Society). UK trademark number 1448790.

Scripture quotations marked NKJV are taken from the New King James Version. Copyright © 1979, 1980, 1982 by Thomas Nelson, Inc. Used by permission. All rights reserved.

First published 2017

British Library Cataloguing-in-Publication Data
A catalogue record for this book is available from the British Library.

ISBN: 978-1-78359-565-5
eBook ISBN: 978-1-78359-566-2

Set in Dante 12/15 pt
Typeset in Great Britain by CRB Associates, Potterhanworth, Lincolnshire
Printed in Great Britain by Ashford Colour Press Ltd, Gosport, Hampshire

Inter-Varsity Press publishes Christian books that are true to the Bible and that communicate the gospel, develop discipleship and strengthen the church for its mission in the world.

IVP originated within the Inter-Varsity Fellowship, now the Universities and Colleges Christian Fellowship, a student movement connecting Christian Unions in universities and colleges throughout Great Britain, and a member movement of the International Fellowship of Evangelical Students. Website: www.uccf.org.uk. That historic association is maintained, and all senior IVP staff and committee members subscribe to the UCCF Basis of Faith.

CONTENTS

FOREWORD

Is it possible to be a good Christian and a successful entrepreneur? This is the subject of the excellent new book you have in your hands. Richard Higginson and Kina Robertshaw discuss how a strong faith in God can be compatible with the job of growing a thriving business, and interviewed fifty Christian entrepreneurs as part of their research.

The Bible explicitly encourages believers to exploit their talents, which must surely include the ability to found and run a business. As it says in Ecclesiastes 9:10, 'Whatsoever thy hand findeth to do, do it with thy might; for there is no work, nor device, nor knowledge, nor wisdom, in the grave, whither thou goest' (AV). Most of the more impressive entrepreneurs I've known, whether religious or not, don't really do it for the money. They build businesses to provide the world with their products and services, to generate jobs and taxes, to contribute productively to society, and to make full use of their God-given abilities. Entrepreneurs often see their work as a calling, rather than just work.

Moreover, entrepreneurs in general display several characteristics which are part of Christian teaching: industriousness, passion, self-improvement, service, stewardship and charity. Indeed, some Christians would argue that God was in a sense the first entrepreneur, since he was the ultimate creator and cultivator. Of course, God was not driven by commercial motives – but he certainly possessed vision and was undoubtedly a risk-taker.

Managing a business using strict Christian ethics cannot be easy. One has to avoid activities which could be considered vices, such as gambling. Staff, competitors and suppliers all have to be treated with respect at all times. That can be hard in the rough-and-tumble, litigious world of business. For example, companies suffer endlessly from crime – in recent weeks, different firms with which I'm involved have experienced a burnt-out vehicle, a robbery and a minor fraud. These troubles have to be dealt with stoically. And there can be no room for any of the deadly sins like pride, envy or greed. Meanwhile, the devil tempts entrepreneurs to pay less tax, indulge in sharp practices or succumb to the sense of power which flows from owning a large enterprise. For a good Christian, all these practices must be stoutly resisted.

A particular nonconformist branch of Christianity which had a remarkable impact on the industrial landscape in Britain was that of the Quakers. Not only did Quakers found the original Lloyds and Barclays banks, but Quakers also started Cadbury's confectionery and Clarks shoes. Considering that, in 1851, there were fewer than 20,000 of them in the entire country, their achievements are proof that culture matters greatly when trying to understand entrepreneurship.

Even in Silicon Valley, the church plays a big role. Of the residents there, 43% belong to a religious institution, showing that there is a strong element of faith even in the centre of the technology industry. Most of the religious locals are Catholic or Evangelical Christians, but there are also plenty of Hindus, Zen Buddhists and Jews. I suspect some of the idealism so prevalent across the tech start-up universe is influenced by the religious beliefs of many in Silicon Valley.

I like doing business with people of faith who are entrepreneurs because they are generally honest and possess integrity. I admire the fact that they work towards a higher calling, other than simply laying up treasures upon this earth (Matthew 6:19), and, by being entrepreneurs, follow the Bible's advice to 'be fruitful, and multiply' (Genesis 1:28 AV).

I commend this book to you as a valuable study of a fascinating cohort of enterprising men and women, and I thank the authors for their efforts in writing it.

Luke Johnson
Chairman, Risk Capital Partners,
and entrepreneurship columnist, *The Sunday Times*

ACKNOWLEDGMENTS

God has graciously sent us some wonderful partners along the way. There are many people we want to thank for their help in writing this book:

First and foremost, the fifty entrepreneurs who kindly made time for us and agreed to be interviewed: David Ball, Jyoti Banerjee, Simon Berry, David Bishop, David Capps, John Carlisle, Mike Clargo, Martin Clark, Brian Clouston, Daniel Cooper, Hugh Davidson, Andrew Glover, Gary Grant, Gordon Haynes, David Henderson, Peter Higginson, Jeremy Higham, Ramona Hirschi, Tony Hodges, Curt Hopkins, Matthew Kimpton-Smith, Valerie King, Simon Lawson, Richard Leftley, Rebeca Li, John Lovatt, Simon Macaulay, Caroline Marsh, Jerry Marshall, Mark Mitchell, Barry Morris, Gareth Mulholland, Keith Noronha, Gavin Oldham, LingLing Parnin, Adrian Patterson, Eric Payne, Andrew Perry, Adair Richards, Natasha Rufus Isaacs, David Runton, David Saunderson, Phil Schluter, Grant Smith, Phil Staunton, Andrew Tanswell, Matthew Turnour, Sir Peter Vardy, Jody Wainwright and Nigel Walter.

In addition:

- the Allchurches Trust and in particular their former Grants and Relationships Manager, Philip Arundel, who offered a generous grant which made it possible for Kina to carry out the fifty interviews;

- Hannah Smith, Rachel Steer, Sandy Waldron, Tony Njamba and Charles Higgins, who all helped in transcribing the recorded interviews;
- our partners Felicity (Richard's wife) and Rory (Kina's husband) for their constant love, support and encouragement;
- Richard's colleagues at Ridley Hall, who stood in for him while he took a term's study leave to write during the summer term of 2016;
- Eve Poole, chair of Faith in Business, who kindly commented on a first draft of the book, and encouraged us both throughout;
- the Rt Revd Peter Forster, Bishop of Chester, who put us on to a very lively network of Christian entrepreneurs in north-west England;
- Steve Mitchell, editor at IVP / SPCK, for his enthusiasm when we first broached the idea for the book, and his careful, patient and detailed work in helping to bring the final text to publication;
- Steve Apted, former General Manager of IVP, who commended us to Steve Mitchell;
- each other, because we have really enjoyed working together on this, and believe that God has given us a 'divine connection';
- Bryony Benier and all involved in the copy-editing and book production process at IVP / SPCK.

Praise be to God. Our prayer is that he will continue to be glorified through the work of Christian entrepreneurs.

Richard Higginson and Kina Robertshaw

INTRODUCTION

This book gives expression to a voice that is not often heard – the voice of Christian entrepreneurs. They are a dynamic, innovative group of people who are making a major contribution to our society through the companies they run, the products they make and the people they influence. *A Voice to Be Heard* celebrates their work, mostly through their own words.

The book is based on interviews with fifty Christian entrepreneurs from a wide variety of business sectors. We begin by providing pen-portraits of five. Then we place their stories in a wider context. In chapter 2 we examine what the Bible has to say about entrepreneurs, considering several biblical characters – God included – who display the marks of an entrepreneur. In chapter 3 we show how the image of entrepreneurs in the UK has changed for the better over the past forty years, and how Christian entrepreneurs are making a major contribution in the Global South. In chapter 4 we explore the noble heritage of distinguished Christian entrepreneurs from previous generations – people who put their faith into action and can still inspire the present generation. Then we explain more about our understanding of the word 'entrepreneur', spell out our research methods and indicate the scope of the questions we asked.

In the remaining chapters we selectively cite material from the interviews, grouped around a series of 'twin themes' that emerged. So we look at calling and kingdom; vision and passion; creativity and courage; relationships and service; stewardship and power; integrity and honesty; prayer and fasting; and perseverance and hope. We examine the tricky issue of the relationship between entrepreneurs and the church. Then we end with what might seem a surprising conclusion, but one that we now hold deeply: that entrepreneurs have the potential to play a major role in the church's *mission*. That is a challenge both for the churches and for the entrepreneurs themselves.

This is a book for actual entrepreneurs, aspiring entrepreneurs and anyone who wants to know more about them. It has been a hugely enjoyable book to research and write: we have met and made friends with so many interesting and inspiring people. We hope you experience the same enjoyment, stimulus and challenge as you read it.

1. FIVE CHRISTIAN ENTREPRENEURS

Gary Grant (Chief Executive, The Entertainer; toy retail)

The Entertainer was founded by Gary Grant and his wife Catherine in 1981, in their home town of Amersham in Buckinghamshire. In 1985 they purchased their second toy shop in nearby Beaconsfield, and in 1991 they opened their third shop in Slough. That was the year in which something very important happened to Gary. He became a Christian. It was a life-changing event.

Gary wondered whether he should remain in his job. He said to an accountant Christian friend, 'I don't think being in business and being a Christian are compatible. Is that right?'

His friend replied, 'They are, but being a Christian and running the business the way that you are may not be compatible.'

In addition, a customer took Gary to task for selling products that were related to Hallowe'en. These conversations led Gary to radically review the way he ran his business.

The Entertainer stopped selling Hallowe'en products on the grounds that they celebrated a pagan ritual connected with the occult.

At a time when Sunday trading laws were being relaxed, Gary also took the bold decision not to open on Sundays. He wanted his staff to be free on Sundays to spend time with their families – and he still does. He now says that The Entertainer sells so many products from Mondays to Saturdays that it does not need to open on Sundays. His staff appreciate the regular rest day and so are motivated to work energetically and enthusiastically.

Gary says that decisions that might look as if they would cost the company money have had the opposite effect. 'In October 1991, when we stopped selling Hallowe'en, we had the most amazing October business that we've ever had. God showed me that he could be trusted.' In 2006–8, when business everywhere was reeling, all of The Entertainer's major competitors – even those that traded seven days a week – went bust. The Entertainer survived, but it was a very close call. Gary called a company prayer meeting to ask for God's help; some of the staff who attended each week were not even Christians.

Gary took no pleasure in competitors' discomfort, but as the upturn came he found himself able to offer jobs to excellent staff who had been made redundant by other companies. Employees ranging from Saturday staff to the accountancy team share bonuses from corporate profits. In addition they receive financial awards for completing various training challenges or giving good customer service.

Gary delights in the joy that the retail sector can bring to people's lives. 'I love crazes, when there is a massive demand for things that really get the adrenalin going. Sometimes I go outside and study the expression on people's faces. I love seeing the delight and pleasure on young children's faces when there is something they really get excited about.'

Consistent with the biblical principle of tithing, The Entertainer donates 10% of its net annual profits to charity each year. It encourages its 1,000 employees to donate a portion of their salary to charity through Workplace Giving, and 42% of the staff do so. The retailer is also a member of the Pennies scheme, whereby customers are given the option to donate a few pence to charity at the till. So if a customer spends £9.75 they typically round the figure up to £10. On average this generates £5,000 of donations each week and The Entertainer has now raised £1 million for charity, much of it for children's hospitals.

The Entertainer is now one of the fastest-growing companies in the UK. In 2015 it opened eighteen new stores, rocketing from 100 to 118. At the time of publication, the latest tally was 136, along with six international stores. The Entertainer has also been named as one of *The Sunday Times* 100 Best Companies to Work For.

David Ball (Chairman, David Ball Group; construction)

Cement plays a vital role in construction as a substance that binds other materials together, notably in the making of concrete. Its manufacture and use have many negative impacts on the environment, producing airborne pollution in the form of dust, gases, noise, vibration and about 5% of global man-made carbon dioxide emissions. But there is now a new concrete available that has been designed with zero cement. Appropriately called Cemfree, it meets the demands of sustainable structural concrete, which are that it should drastically reduce concrete's carbon dioxide legacy, provide greater durability, require less steel reinforcement and demand less water.

The company that has invented and pioneered Cemfree is the David Ball Group, situated at Bourn, a small village nine miles outside Cambridge. It employs just over sixty people and has an annual turnover of £5.5 million, currently growing at 20% a year. The company was founded in 1970 by David Ball, then a young engineering graduate from Northern Ireland. David started his career with another cement company but fell foul of the managing director because of his confidence in proposing solutions to technical problems. Finding himself out of a job, but continuing to experiment with ingredients and making product samples in his kitchen sink, David set up his own company and won a contract with cement manufacturer Blue Circle. He has never really looked back.

Throughout its history, the company has been at the forefront of technological improvements. In the 1990s, the David Ball Group took the performance of integrally waterproof concrete to a new level as it reformulated PUDLO, the world's first commercial concrete waterproofing mixture. Re-engineering it around modern architectural needs, David Ball used PUDLO in projects such as refurbishment works at the Royal Albert Hall and the creation of the spectacular Dubai Fountains.

David came to faith under the influence of his parents and has always sought to apply it to his work. He believes that his business contributes to the building of God's kingdom. He is driven by three key concerns: 'The first is a passion for quality, making sure the product is right first time, every time. The second is training and education of our staff, along with the training of our customers into the way things work properly. The third is service, service above self. You put the interest of your customer and your client first.' He believes that commitment to these high standards enhances the quality of life and brings glory to God.

The company is accredited with ISO 9001 and 14001, international manufacturing standards which regulate the industry. As a young man David was initially sceptical about these systems. He was influenced by his mother who regarded such bureaucracy as 'the mark of the beast', mentioned in the book of Revelation. But David came to appreciate the value of the ISO. It helped to increase production, reduced defects to zero, won the company government contracts and inspired customer confidence.

David is now in his early seventies. He is less hands-on within the company, but still its owner and chairman. He has become a highly respected figure within the industrial sands, cements and concrete industry. For many years he chaired the Christian organization Chaplaincy to People at Work, which has provided pastoral care for employees in the Cambridge area.

Mark Mitchell (Group Managing Director, Mitchell Group; car dealership)

Mark Mitchell is a born salesman. At the age of seven, he discovered that if he put two hamsters together in a cage, they multiplied quickly. He then took the baby hamsters to school and sold them for 10p each. By the age of fourteen he had secured a loan of £50 from a bank to start a motorcycle business, initially selling the bikes at the gates of his senior school. Mark says, 'I was too young to ride them, but I bought them from the local paper, and my dad brought them up to school for me. That was when I first became a dealer.'

Mark came from a Christian home, attending St Mary's Upton on the Wirral, Cheshire. As youngsters, he and his brothers gave the Sunday school teachers 'so much grief: we were inattentive and I guess quite obnoxious. Most weeks we were bringing various items of livestock – some alive, some dead – anything to take the focus off the week's Bible story!' But at the age of eleven, Mark went away on a children's camp and embarked on a personal relationship with Jesus Christ: '1 June 1973 was an evening I clearly remember as the day I decided to follow Jesus Christ and live as his disciple.'

For Mark the urge to sell things, especially objects on wheels, remained strong. While studying economics at Leeds University, he and his friends sold 200 motorbikes in an academic year from their student accommodation. After graduating he worked for Austin Rover and then Ford for several years, harbouring ambitions to run his own company while building up the experience that would equip him to do so.

In 1988 Mark met his future wife and business partner Anita at St Michael-le-Belfrey Church in York. In 1991 the couple invested £50 each to buy a dormant company 'off the shelf' and then raised a bank loan of £10,000 to invest in their first petrol service station in Warrington. Soon they had four petrol stations. By 1996 Mark had enough capital to buy a car dealership franchise from Mitsubishi Motors, operating from Eastham in Cheshire. A franchise with Lexus followed.

Like Gary Grant, Mark has taken a stand on Sunday trading. In the entrance to the main Mitchell Group complex, a sign says the opening times are Monday to Saturday, but this is followed by 'Sunday. At home with the family'. This led to a parting of the ways with Mitsubishi in 2004. The Japanese company stipulated that Sunday trading was mandatory in an area in which the majority of surrounding car dealers were open for business. 'Given the circumstances,' Mark says, 'I had no choice. I couldn't keep Lexus closed while opening Mitsubishi.' At the same time, he says, 'I had no wish to run

Mitsubishi down, nor would I ever want to legislate about the Sunday-shopping habits of others.' He received 150 letters of support from customers for his principled stance.

Mark also planned for the future. He sought and obtained new franchises with Mazda and Skoda. The Mitchell Group's five-acre complex at Cheshire Oaks is now the home of Lexus Chester, Mitchell Mazda and Mitchell Skoda. The Group has a turnover approaching £50 million and a dedicated staff of 100 people.

Mark is not reticent about sharing his Christian faith. Each Christmas the Mitchell Group celebrates a carol service with about 1,200 of its customers in Chester Cathedral. Mark says, 'Customers are invited to sing carols and hear the gospel presented gently and sensitively.' Men's groups from across the region visit for a 'Men and Motors' evening. After they have driven a range of flagship models and enjoyed a 'behind the scenes' tour of the premises, a Chinese banquet and drinks are served in the boardroom. The scene turns into an open forum and Mark has 'the opportunity to reflect on some of life's challenges and the joys of being a Christian. I'm constantly amazed at how these "no-holds-barred" times prompt immense openness from so many of these guys, who would struggle to raise issues in other settings.' This is effective Christian witness.

Val King (Managing Director, Rooflight; architecture and construction)

The use of lighting in roofs is fairly recent. The first use of roof-lighting on a large scale occurred in huge Victorian buildings such as railway stations, corn exchanges and the Crystal Palace of 1850. Yet a bird's-eye view of any modern town or city shows it has become an important feature of our buildings.

In the early 1990s, Oxfordshire architect Peter King took the original Victorian cast-iron design and modified it. He innovated the Conservation Rooflight – a high thermal performance, hinged, double-glazed steel unit that sat discreetly flush with the skyline. The design won approval from fellow architects. In 1996 the Rooflight Company was born.

The managing director is Peter's wife Val. She is an energetic and resourceful woman who has led the company through highs and lows. It is now set on an upward curve. Based at Shipton-under-Wychwood in rural Oxfordshire, the Rooflight Company employs over seventy people and has a turnover of nearly £8 million. The company supports several charities regularly, donating 10% of Rooflight's profits. It works closely with the Nasio Trust, which supports orphaned children in Western Kenya, providing them with a daily meal, education and medical care. The company has also raised funds to protect people from malaria in Malawi. The provision of nets allows adults and children to avoid harmful insect bites and sleep more safely at night.

For Val, the impact of Christian faith upon her work is mainly in the area of values. The company has articulated a clear and straightforward set of values:

- Integrity – We expect integrity in all our interactions with one another, customers and suppliers.
- Care – We care about what we do and how it affects our customers, suppliers and one another, and have a genuine interest in everyone's development. We care about people less fortunate and help them.
- Empowerment – We are humble enough to recognize that we are often not the best person or team to do a particular job, so we find out who is and empower them.

- Unity – No-one stands alone: we work together and respect one another's contribution. Cross-functional teams are the norm here.

'The four values are the touchstone of our company. We regularly question our approach to a problem and revise it in the light of one of the values,' says Val. 'This helps us get to the heart of the problem and develop a solution that everyone buys into. I firmly believe business can be a "Force for Good"; people want to be part of something that is not just material output, but a community of people trying to make the world a better place.' Roof windows help to create beautifully designed, naturally lit environments.

Val sees a positive mental attitude as really important. 'If you create a positive environment, that's a good thing and I'm sure God would want that.' She takes inspiration from business guru Charles Handy, who says the companies that survive longest are those that make a unique offering to the world: 'Not just growth or money, but their excellence, their respect for others or their ability to make people happy. Some call these things a soul.'

Matthew Kimpton-Smith (Managing Director, Cygnet Group; engineering)

In a family business, sons and daughters often take over from their father or mother. They may walk straight into the business in their early twenties. Alternatively, the younger generation may serve their apprenticeship in larger firms and broaden their experience before returning to the family fold. That is the pattern followed by Matthew Kimpton-Smith.

Matthew studied Economics at Cambridge University in the 1980s and worked as an accountant with Price Waterhouse and BOC, before feeling led to join the family business, the Cygnet Group, in 1996. Along the way he became a Christian, coming to faith through an Alpha course.

Cygnet grew out of a textiles company, Texkimp, founded in 1974 by Matthew's grandfather Bill Kimpton and his father Colin Smith. It was then based at Quarry Bank Mill, near Manchester Airport; Matthew remembers being allowed to turn on the Styal waterwheel as a boy.

As the UK textile industry went into decline, the company became increasingly involved in the export business and started to produce machines for technical and high-performance fibres for the growing global market. By the time Matthew became Group Managing Director in 2006, Texkimp was one of several companies in an interconnected group, operating under the new name Cygnet. Matthew sought to give the group a serenity and stability signified by the image of a swan. In recent years, Cygnet has specialized in two strategic areas: the production and processing of technical fibres, and oil and gas technology. It is certainly flourishing. Cygnet was awarded The Queen's Award for International Trade for outstanding overseas sales growth in 2014. In three years it experienced overseas earnings growth of 255% and almost doubled the number of employees.

The juxtaposition of home and overseas focus characterizes the activities of the Cygnet Group. Today 96% of its sales are for export, with products destined for thirty different countries. But virtually all Cygnet's manufacturing is done in the UK, predominantly in the north-west and by other, smaller companies. This puts good relationships with other stake-holders – foreign customers on the one hand, and domestic suppliers on the other – at an absolute premium.

This is an area where Matthew excels. He rates emotional intelligence highly as one of the characteristics that has most contributed to the company's success. He loves interaction with other people.

Cygnet's mission statement is 'Empowering our people to deliver engineering excellence'. The company's five key values are:

- treating others as we wish to be treated ourselves (a clear echo of the Golden Rule articulated by Jesus in Matthew 7:12);
- actively listening to one another;
- working as a team where every success is a team success;
- having the utmost respect for the people we work with;
- being open and honest in all our dealings.

When new employees join Cygnet, Matthew spends one-to-one time with them talking through these values, making sure they embrace them wholeheartedly. But he does not look for dull uniformity among his staff. He recognizes that God has made each person unique. 'It is important to maximize what God has given you and go with it,' he says. He appreciates that some people are introverts and others are extroverts; both have important contributions to make. At the same time, both types can usefully 'borrow' from the other to some degree. So he nurtures introverts who learn to be outgoing in certain situations, and extroverts who learn to be quiet and listen when the occasion demands. At Cygnet, both manufacturing processes and personal skills are constantly being honed and finessed.

Matthew is committed to his local church, and has no inhibitions about saying so on the company website. But he has come to have greater expectations of community or fellowship within his own workforce than from a typical congregation. Where staff are fully aligned in pursuing a corporate vision, the depth of relationship and unity of purpose can be remarkable.

In 2016 Matthew had a serious accident. He suffered a cardiac arrest while riding his bike, cracked his skull in two places and was in a coma for a while. Happily, he is now making a good recovery, which has amazed his doctors. He also has a strong sense of the Lord's hand being on the business over this period; other staff have stepped up to the mark while he has been away.

Christian entrepreneurs

What do these five people – Gary, David, Mark, Val and Matthew – have in common? Clearly they are all successful businesspeople and they all happen to be Christians. But there is a more specific answer than that. They are all Christian *entrepreneurs*.

What is an entrepreneur? The obvious answer is that it is someone who is the founder, head and majority owner of a company. But this is not quite accurate. Four of the businesspeople we have discussed played a prominent part in founding their companies. One, Matthew, did not (the family firm already existed), but few would begrudge him the title of entrepreneur. In addition, we are not convinced that people who start companies that are indistinguishable from their competitors – 'me too' companies – genuinely deserve the accolade of entrepreneur. Entrepreneurs offer something new or different. The novelty may consist in the product, method of production, niche market or corporate structure. Entrepreneurs pursue commercial success and are innovators. Our chosen five all qualify on that score. We shall define the word 'entrepreneur' more precisely in chapter 5.

Our chosen five are also *Christian* entrepreneurs. By this we mean more than entrepreneurs who happen to be Christian. It is possible to run a company in a way that makes little connection with the faith one affirms. But these are Christians who see their companies as an outworking of their faith. They are united by a desire to bring glory to God, to serve their fellow humans and to set their companies in a context of prayer.

Gary, David, Mark, Val and Matthew are five out of fifty Christian entrepreneurs interviewed in the process of writing this book. They are some of the more successful, high-profile and long-lasting among our sample. Their achievements are worthy of celebration and there are lessons to be learnt from this success. However, we know that business success can be fleeting, and we have not restricted our survey to well-known Christian businesspeople. We have deliberately interviewed entrepreneurs at many different stages of their careers: the young, the middle aged and those embarking on retirement. The verdict is still out on how successful some will prove to be. Business is full of ups and downs, with sudden crises and reversals interrupting periods of steady growth. Nor are all Christian entrepreneurs as confident about expressing their faith as those profiled in this first chapter. We have sought to portray people in their doubts and uncertainties as well as parading their strong convictions.

Our research has convinced us of this: there is a wealth of entrepreneurial activity and talent among Christians in the UK. We have been excited and encouraged to find so many businesspeople of genuine faith with interesting ideas, determined to implement them – to give them a go. However, this wealth of entrepreneurial activity is not something that most people know about. We have written this book to celebrate the work of Christian entrepreneurs, to draw it to public attention and to encourage Christian entrepreneurs in what they are trying to do. Theirs indeed is *a voice to be heard*.

Richard and Kina

At this stage, it may be helpful to say something about our own stories.

Richard is a theological educator. At Ridley Hall he combines the roles of Lecturer in Christian Ethics and Director of Studies with Director of Faith in Business. This project, which began under the name 'God on Monday', makes positive connections between Christian faith and the business world. It encourages and equips Christians in business to be faithful followers of Jesus in what we know can often be difficult and demanding working contexts.

In the course of running Faith in Business, Richard has taken on projects of an entrepreneurial nature. Every spring since 2000, he has organized and run a weekend conference exploring a topical business theme from a Christian perspective, during which fifty or sixty businessmen and women converge on Ridley Hall for forty-eight hours of stimulating input and invigorating fellowship. Recent conference themes have included Motivation in Business, Dilemmas in Business and The Life Cycle of Business. Faith in Business has also co-published a quarterly journal, *Faith in Business*, for the past twenty years. This provides an opportunity for business-people, academics and church leaders to write about business. Under Richard's leadership, Ridley Hall has made a sustained and unique contribution to resourcing Christians in the business world.

Kina's experience is very different. She grew up in Zambia, one of a large family of twelve. At the age of ten, inspired by her instinctively entrepreneurial mother, Kina and her cousin sold peanuts at the gate of her father's house. Leaving school at sixteen, she developed an interest in fashion and worked in retail stores in Johannesburg and London. There she carefully observed the ingredients and working habits that support success in retail, hoping that she would in time have the opportunity to run her own fashion business.

In due course, Kina did set up her first store in Lusaka, and then opened a second store in Johannesburg. Then the opportunity arose to set up the first independent department store in Zambia. She rose to the challenge, and went on to expand the business into complementary areas linking with the Zambian fashion and music industry. She established an events agency, published fashion and music magazines and set up a recording and music management company. Kina was nominated Zambian Businesswoman of the Year in 2009.

Relocating with her family to England in 2008, the re-awakening of Kina's faith led to a desire to study theology. She enrolled at Ridley as an independent student in 2010 and was eventually ordained in 2016. During her studies she reflected on her past experience, writing a dissertation on Christian entrepreneurship under Richard's supervision. She then wanted to take this work a stage further, to interview Christian entrepreneurs and discover what motivates them and makes them tick. What is it that inspires entrepreneurs, frustrates them, challenges them and brings them joy? This curiosity led to the research which lies behind this book.

Richard and Kina have collaborated on this every step of the way. While Kina did most of the interviews and Richard did most of the writing, it is very much a joint venture. We hope what follows informs and inspires you.

2. 'SHE MAKES LINEN GARMENTS AND SELLS THEM'

So what does the Bible have to say about entrepreneurship?

Clearly, 'entrepreneur' is a word that postdates the Bible. There is no precise equivalent in either Old Testament Hebrew or New Testament Greek. Similarly, the 'company' in anything like the structural form we know it today did not exist in biblical times. But the production of goods, the provision of services, the trading of materials and the consumption of resources all took place, then as now. The Bible contains a wide cast of characters who span a full range of occupations. Several of these display characteristics we would call entrepreneurial.

Let's start by looking at four biblical characters who have more than a hint of entrepreneur about them. Then we shall turn our attention to God and discover an entrepreneurial God right at the heart of the biblical narrative.

Jacob – an entrepreneur in the shadows

One of the clearest examples of a person with entrepreneurial flair in Scripture is the patriarch Jacob. He was adept in animal husbandry – the management and care of animals in which genetic qualities and behaviour considered advantageous to humans are developed. But he operated in a rather 'shady' way. Bill Bolton and John Thompson, authors of a notable book called *Entrepreneurs*, describe Jacob as 'a classic example of the Arthur Daley car salesman type of entrepreneur'. The story of his dealings in Genesis 30 and 31 is worth examining in some detail.

Without doubt there was a cunning streak to Jacob's character. As a young man he cheated his slightly older twin brother Esau, pretending to be his brother and obtaining from their blind father Isaac the blessing that Isaac intended for Esau. Incurring Esau's enmity and fleeing for his life, Jacob ended up with his uncle Laban in Haran and fell in love with Laban's beautiful younger daughter Rachel. However, the cheat met his match in Laban. Laban made Jacob work seven years for his bride and then surreptitiously gave him his elder daughter Leah, who was decidedly less attractive. Jacob had to work a further seven years for Rachel, and after that he suffered the frustration of Leah's being far more fertile than Rachel.

The work Jacob did for Laban was looking after flocks of sheep and goats. When Jacob stated his desire to return home, Laban tried to dissuade him. Jacob asked Laban to give him all the speckled and spotted sheep, every black lamb and all the spotted and speckled goats: 'such shall be my wages' (Genesis 30:32). It appears that these distinctive animals were more highly valued. Laban consented to this arrangement, but then reneged on it; he removed all the speckled and spotted sheep and goats and gave them to his sons.

Jacob responded not by confronting Laban, but by resorting to some innovative veterinary methods. Genesis 30:37–40 tells us:

Then Jacob took fresh rods of poplar and almond and plane, and peeled white streaks in them, exposing the white of the rods. He set the rods that he had peeled in front of the flocks in the troughs, that is, the watering places, where the flocks came to drink. And since they bred when they came to drink, the flocks bred in front of the rods, and so the flocks produced young that were striped, speckled, and spotted.

Jacob kept these lambs for himself and separated them from Laban's flock. The net outcome was that Jacob's flock were the stronger animals, Laban's the feebler, and Jacob 'grew exceedingly rich' (Genesis 30:43).

What is going on here? Was Jacob invoking some magical or superstitious ideas to breed the animals he wanted? Or had he observed that in some mysterious way the breeding environment of animals affects the appearance of their off-spring? Later on (Genesis 31:10–13) Jacob told his two wives Rachel and Leah that during the mating of the flock he had a dream in which he 'looked up and saw that the male goats that leaped upon the flock were striped, speckled, and mottled'. An angel of the Lord pointed this out to Jacob, saying, 'I have seen all that Laban is doing to you.' What is uncertain is when Jacob had this dream. Did he carry out his plan in response to the dream, or did the dream serve to confirm what he had already done?

There was a curious combination of attributes in Jacob. He gave God the credit for his success (e.g. Genesis 31:9, 42), but he was also a habitual schemer. In his relationship with Laban, he was probably more sinned against than sinning. He had been badly treated by his uncle, and was determined to outwit him. It is a scenario that often recurs in business. Jesus' words to his disciples reverberate with many entrepreneurs:

'I am sending you out like sheep in the midst of wolves; so be wise as serpents and innocent as doves' (Matthew 10:16). Jacob was as wise as a serpent; it is less clear that he was as innocent as a dove. His story also shows that, though family businesses can often work successfully, they have potential pitfalls. Jacob and Laban's ability to work together harmoniously was complicated by difficult family dynamics: namely Jacob's upbringing and the grievance he felt towards Laban over his handling of Jacob's wedding arrangements. A dysfunctional family makes for acrimonious business relationships. But God does not abandon individuals in these situations; in a mysterious way, things can work together for good (Romans 8:28). He had a special purpose in view for Jacob and his family, and caused him to prosper.

Nehemiah – a brilliant project manager

Nehemiah was not an entrepreneur. There is no hint that a desire for commercial gain underlay his various activities. He has passed into biblical history as a project manager *par excellence*, the man responsible for the rebuilding of the wall of Jerusalem in the fifth century BC. This followed his appointment as governor of Judah by the Persian king Artaxerxes. But he displayed many notable entrepreneurial characteristics, and there is much that Christian entrepreneurs today can learn from him.

First, Nehemiah's actions were grounded in prayer – prayer which came out of heartfelt emotion. An exile in Babylon, he was distressed when he received news from Jerusalem that the survivors there were in great trouble and shame, the wall of Jerusalem was broken down and its gates had been destroyed by fire (Nehemiah 1:3). Nehemiah's response was to weep, mourn, fast and pray, over a period of several days.

Second, out of this prayer emerged the vision of a rebuilt city, and with that a plan. Nehemiah was cupbearer to the king, and he resolved to take his life in his hands, showing great courage in approaching Artaxerxes, explaining the situation and asking permission to go and rebuild Jerusalem. The king responded positively and gave him letters of permission to ease his way (Nehemiah 2:1–10). Once back in Jerusalem, Nehemiah carried out a careful and thorough reconnaissance, establishing how he would tackle the work.

Third, Nehemiah showed an ability to motivate the demoralized people of Jerusalem. He explained his plan and their response was unexpectedly upbeat: 'Then they said, "Let us start building!" So they committed themselves to the common good' (Nehemiah 2:18). Nehemiah involved some unlikely people in the heavy work of making repairs and building the wall: goldsmiths (3:8, 31), perfumers (3:8) and priests (3:28). The rapidity and intensity with which the work was done is evident from two succinct reports:

So we rebuilt the wall, and all the wall was joined together to half its height; for the people had a mind to work.
(Nehemiah 4:6)

So the wall was finished on the twenty-fifth day of the month Elul, in fifty-two days.
(Nehemiah 6:15)

Not everyone liked what Nehemiah was up to. The Jews had their enemies, people who lived in the vicinity and preferred to see the inhabitants of Jerusalem in a state of disarray. Sanballat, Tobiah and Geshem did their best to disrupt Nehemiah's plans and invited him to a meeting where they doubtless meant him harm (Nehemiah 6:1). But Nehemiah showed shrewdness in discerning their intentions and resilience in thwarting them.

Above all, Nehemiah showed great faith in God. He told his opponents: 'The God of heaven is the one who will give us success, and we his servants are going to start building' (2:20). The workers took practical precautionary measures (they all had tools in one hand and weapons in the other), but Nehemiah inspired them with the words, 'Our God will fight for us' (4:16–20). The neighbouring peoples were forced to acknowledge that 'this work had been accomplished with the help of our God' (6:16).

Prayer, vision, courage, planning, motivation of others, shrewdness, resilience, faith: these are all characteristics that entrepreneurs need. Nehemiah is an inspiring role model for people in many walks of life, not just for congregations involved in a church building project!

Lydia – the dealer in purple

We cannot be sure whether Lydia was an entrepreneur or simply a trader. This is what Luke, writing about his time with Paul in Philippi, says about her:

> On the sabbath day we went outside the gate by the river, where we supposed there was a place of prayer; and we sat down and spoke to the women who had gathered there. A certain woman named Lydia, a worshipper of God, was listening to us; she was from the city of Thyatira and a dealer in purple cloth. The Lord opened her heart to listen eagerly to what was said by Paul.
> (Acts 16:13–14)

Thyatira was famous as a centre for purple dye, which came from shellfish. It was a widely desired commodity, bought for a high price. Lydia sold clothes treated with the dye. Purple fabric was valuable and expensive; it was often worn as a sign of royalty or nobility. Lydia's home city Thyatira was 240 miles from Philippi, in what is now Turkey, in the province of Lydia, from where she may have derived her name.

It sounds as if Lydia had settled in Philippi rather than just being a passing trader, because she had a house there. Luke tells us, 'When she and her household were baptized, she urged us, saying, "If you have judged me to be faithful to the Lord, come and stay at my home." And she prevailed upon us' (Acts 16:15). When Paul and Silas got into trouble and were imprisoned but then released, they went to Lydia's home and spent time there.

Lydia must have been a confident woman of independent spirit to invite some foreign men whom she hardly knew to stay in her house. This suggests that she was an influential merchant, accustomed to taking a leading role in a business setting. She must also have had a fair-sized house, large enough for others to congregate there. So she may well have been an entrepreneur, perhaps the leading seller of purple dye in Philippi. Already a convert to worship of the Jewish God, Lydia had a heart open to listen eagerly to the good news Paul preached about Jesus. This open heart was paralleled by her open house. She embodies the virtue of hospitality.

The virtuous wife – entrepreneur extraordinaire

It is actually a nameless individual in the Bible who fits most precisely the definition of entrepreneur. The final section of the book of Proverbs (31:10–31) is a paean of praise to a 'capable wife' or 'virtuous woman'. She is in fact so impressive and multi-talented that we may wonder whether she is a real person; perhaps she is a composite picture of ideal womanhood.

THE VIRTUOUS WIFE | 23

Although a wife and mother, the main focus of the writer's attention falls on her economic productivity. Indeed, it is precisely through her business acumen that she serves her family and extended household so well.

Here we have the epitome of a thriving family business, with this impressive woman clearly at the helm:

> She seeks wool and flax,
>> and works with willing hands.
> She is like the ships of the merchant,
>> she brings her food from far away.
> She rises while it is still night
>> and provides food for her household
>> and tasks for her servant-girls.
> She considers a field and buys it;
>> with the fruit of her hands she plants a vineyard.
> She girds herself with strength,
>> and makes her arms strong.
> She perceives that her merchandise is profitable.
>> Her lamp does not go out at night.
> She puts her hands to the distaff,
>> and her hands hold the spindle.
> (Proverbs 31:13–19)

This capable wife clearly has many strings to her bow. She is adept at property purchase, food purchase and agricultural cultivation. But the focal point of her activity is textiles. This gives her serene confidence that she can provide for her family:

> She is not afraid for her household when it snows,
>> for all her household are clothed in crimson.
> She makes herself coverings;
>> her clothing is fine linen and purple . . .

> She makes linen garments and sells them;
>   she supplies the merchant with sashes.
> Strength and dignity are her clothing,
>   and she laughs at the time to come.
> (Proverbs 31:21–22, 24–25)

However, this laughter is not at others' expense. 'She opens her hand to the poor, and she reaches out her hands to the needy' (31:20). No wonder her children call her happy, and her husband praises her.

We interviewed Rebeca, a London fashion designer who comes from China. She is inspired by the passage above:

> A lot of people might think fashion is superficial, intimidating or nonsense. I had that view at some point. But then I read Proverbs 31. It seems to me that this devout woman is entrepreneurial. She considers a field and buys it. She is also working in fashion or textiles. There are references to spindles, sashes, fabrics. Yet God calls her a virtuous woman.

This impressive woman who combines business virtue with family commitment is a particular inspiration for black Christian women, a fact that reflects the increasingly prominent role women play in the small-business sector of the global economy. The overwhelming majority of loans made by micro-finance organizations – worldwide 75% – go to women, most running micro-enterprises from home. This is because women are much less likely to waste the loans than men; they are better at providing moral support for one another as fellow recipients of loans; and their repayment rates are higher.

While the virtuous woman of Proverbs 31 seems to be more prosperous and privileged than most women in the

Global South today (her husband was 'known in the city gates, taking his seat among the elders of the land', 31:23), the home-based business that she runs bears similarities to theirs. It is not surprising that she inspires their attempts to climb out of poverty. But her many virtues – resourcefulness, hard work, technical skill, wisdom in investment – are ones we can all emulate, black or white, male or female.

God – the original entrepreneur

All these biblical models, however, fall short of a true theology of entrepreneurship. For that we must turn to the trinitarian God. God is the original entrepreneur.

To call God an entrepreneur may sound silly or strange: it provokes that reaction in some people. We use the word in a metaphorical sense; it is not a complete or precise description. Note that the Bible uses numerous occupational images in talking about God. In his book *God the Worker*, Australian theologian Robert Banks lists sixteen such images which he clusters in pairs: composer and performer; metalworker and potter; garment-maker and dresser; gardener and orchardist; farmer and winemaker; shepherd and pastoralist; tentmaker and camper; builder and architect.

Among these images, two in particular speak of God's activity as creator and incorporate activities familiar to an entrepreneur. As a *potter*, God 'moulds' and 'forms'. The God who created the heavens 'formed the earth and made it' (Isaiah 45:18). God forms the animals and birds out of the ground (Genesis 2:19). Above all, he moulds human beings, prompting the confession: 'Yet, O LORD, you are our Father; we are the clay, and you are our potter; we are all the work of your hand' (Isaiah 64:8). In Jeremiah 18 and 19, the potter image is also used of God's prerogative to remake the clay and break the pot. He has the right and ability to make something new.

Remember David Ball, moulding cement anew at his kitchen sink. He took existing products and, seeing their limitations, recast them into something better. That is an entrepreneur working in his heavenly Father's image.

God is also portrayed as a *gardener* in Genesis 2. The description of the garden of Eden speaks wonders of God's love of beauty and generous provision: the trees were 'pleasant to the sight and good for food' (Genesis 2:9). But gardens too get spoilt. The consequence of our fallen condition is a cursed ground that produces thorns and thistles (Genesis 3:17–18). Isaiah compares the nation of Israel to a devoured vineyard (3:14) that produces wild grapes (5:4).

We interviewed Brian, a landscape architect. He had worked in north-east England where 'large tracts of countryside and urban landscape were disfigured by huge coal tips, abandoned steel and chemical works. My vision was to use my training and gifts to heal this despoiled land. My company was part of the team which designed the reclamation works for the first garden festival site in Liverpool.'

The fact that the word 'entrepreneur' is – strictly speaking – unbiblical need not deter us from using it about God. Like Banks, we think that the explicit occupational images used in Scripture about God should not exhaust our talk about him. We can make other comparisons from contemporary work environments. By disciplined use of the imagination we can communicate aspects of God's character in fresh and meaningful ways. Different occupational metaphors provide helpful insights; by taking them together we can build up a coherent understanding of God and what he is like.

Clearly the comparison between God and entrepreneur – as we have defined it – fails in one important respect. Most analogies break down at some point, and this is no exception. God does not commercialize innovation. He is not into making money, though he is concerned about creating wealth in the broader sense. But there are many entrepreneurial qualities which *are* true of God, notably those of vision and creativity.

A visionary, creative, risk-taking God

Visionaries conceive of alternative realities. God did so on an extraordinary scale. He conceived of a world that did not exist, and brought it into being. Ridley colleague Michael Volland describes God's creation of time and space as 'a supreme act of wisdom, imagination and originality'.

The metanarrative of Scripture shows us God's vision for the whole of human history. It tells us the story of creation, fall, the history of Israel, redemption through Jesus, the birth of the Christian church and the consummation at the end of time. This is an overarching vision which puts all that humans do into perspective and makes sense of what we do. Every episode in the biblical story of salvation has something important, challenging and hopeful to say about the practice of business.

God is creative. The first sentence of the Bible tells us that God 'created' (Genesis 1:1). We then see God creating the world in a very measured, ordered and imaginative way. At each stage of the process God pronounces his work 'good'; at the end he pronounces it to be '*very* good' (Genesis 1:12, 18, 21, 24, 31). God takes justifiable satisfaction in the creation which has taken shape around him.

However, God's creativity is not limited to his original act of creating the world. He is a God who habitually delights in making things new. In Isaiah 43:19 God predicts that he is about to do 'a new thing', in relation to his bringing his chosen people back from exile and restoring them. His intervention in the person of Jesus is compared to putting new wine into fresh wineskins (Mark 2:22). On the day of Pentecost, God does a new thing by pouring out his Spirit on all flesh (Acts 2:17). The consummation at the end of time will involve his creating 'a new heaven and a new earth' (Revelation 21:1), fulfilling a promise made in Isaiah 65:17.

God and entrepreneurs also share a willingness to take risks. Indeed, some have defined entrepreneurship principally in these terms. Starting a business involves risking reputation and resources, not knowing the outcome with any assurance.

God did not create a static creation. He created a world where he knew there would be growth and development. As Richard Goossen and Paul Stevens observe, 'That is true of inanimate creation and non-human living creatures.' But it was also true of the riskiest aspect of God's creation: human beings. Goossen and Stevens write:

> God placed the man and woman in a garden of opportunity – but God did not determine what they were to do with it. He did not control them . . . He placed them in a world where everything was open to change, and he took the risk that they would fail.

In many respects human beings did fail. This will not have been a surprise to God, but it was a severe disappointment.

Nevertheless, from the outset God had a back-up plan – the plan of redemption. He put that plan into stunning effect in the person of Jesus. Again, there is something entrepreneurial about this. Most entrepreneurs find that things do not work out precisely according to plan. They are forced to adapt, to revise their calculations, to come up with an alternative strategy which makes good what was missing in the original one. Risk-taking is drastically reduced where an entrepreneur has an excellent contingency plan. Putting it into action is at one and the same time a demonstration of foresight and wisdom, and a mark of dedication and perseverance.

Made in God's image

Christians believe that all human beings are made in the image of God. We all resemble God in certain respects; we all bear his imprint. God is a worker (the word 'work' is used of God's act of creation in Genesis 2:4) and one way in which we mirror or resemble God is through working ourselves.

We believe that entrepreneurs 'image' God in particular ways. They display his characteristics of vision, creativity and risk-taking to an unusual degree. This does not make them superior to other people, but it does suggest they have an important role to play in the fulfilment of God's purposes. Because it is so important – because entrepreneurs have the power to impact others' lives in a major way – we need to carry out that commission in a Christ-like way. We need to be conformed to the image of God's Son (Romans 8:29), the perfect example of what it means to be made in the image of God (Colossians 1:15). We need to be living lives of faithful obedience as Jesus did, in order that we exercise our entrepreneurial gifts in a way that is pleasing to God.

3. ENTREPRENEURS EMERGE

Entrepreneurs used to have a bad reputation in the UK. They were seen as dangerous visionaries, rather like the Pied Piper of Hamelin who lured others to destruction. Driven by the dictates of their own ego, they were impatient to acquire wealth and ready to take moral short cuts. They were ruthless in seeking to eliminate their competitors.

This was the image of entrepreneurs that prevailed forty years ago, when Richard Branson started on his business career. In his autobiography *Business Stripped Bare*, he writes:

> In the 1970s, when we set up Virgin Records, no one in the UK used the word 'entrepreneur' any more. Or if they did, they considered it unsavoury. A businessman running a number of firms was seen as a 'chancer' – the television comic stereotype was Del Boy, the wheeler-dealer on the outside of the law, in *Only Fools and Horses*, or *Minder*'s Arthur Daley, the gin-drinking spiv played brilliantly by

George Cole. In the early days, I was regularly dismissed
as a 'Del Boy' myself . . .

The 1980s and 1990s continued to throw up some real-life
entrepreneurs who appeared to confirm the stereotype. They
operated 'in the shadows', to use the phrase coined by Bolton
and Thompson. These shadowy entrepreneurs were incompe-
tent, dishonest or a mixture of the two, and responsible for
the loss of huge sums of money.

Entrepreneurs in the shadows

John DeLorean was a flamboyant American businessman who
rose through the ranks of the car industry. In the mid-1970s
he resigned from his job at General Motors and announced
his vision for an innovative and radical new car built at a state-
of-the-art production facility. This dream car would be made
of stainless steel and feature distinctive doors shaped as gull
wings, hinged at the top. DeLorean secured $175m to finance
the venture and obtained permission from the Labour government to build the car in Northern Ireland. Car production
started in 1980, but lasted only two years; the company went
into receivership in 1982. Although the car was popular with
some, the niche market DeLorean identified was too small to
meet the rapidly escalating costs. The DMC-12 also compared
unfavourably with sports coupés with more powerful engines
and lower price tags built by competitors. DeLorean's reputation was further tarnished when he was charged with
attempting to broker a $24m cocaine deal in his efforts to raise
money. He was acquitted on the grounds of police entrap-
ment, but his career as an entrepreneur was effectively over.

Robert Maxwell's original name was Jan Hoch. Born a Jew
in what is now the Czech Republic, he emigrated to England

and served in the Pioneer Corps with distinction during the Second World War. He then went into publishing and established his own company, Pergamon Press, while also serving as a Labour MP from 1964 to 1970. But when he tried to merge Pergamon with an American publisher, a Department of Trade and Industry (DTI) inquiry concluded that he had overstated profits through creative accounting practices and that 'he could not be relied on to exercise proper stewardship of a public company'. Nevertheless, he remained in control at Pergamon and the publishing company grew rapidly during the 1970s. In the early 1980s he acquired both Oxford United Football Club and the *Daily Mirror*. Maxwell's commercial empire grew increasingly complex, with his many companies regularly trading in one another's shares and inflating their worth. But as the underlying weakness of this business empire became evident, Maxwell resorted to desperate measures. He secretly transferred shares held by the Mirror Group Pension Fund and pledged them as collateral for further loans. While a BBC *Panorama* team was starting to uncover his dubious activities, news came through of his unexpected death: his naked body was found floating in the sea alongside his private yacht near the Canary Islands.

The stories of DeLorean and Maxwell may be exceptional, but they highlight problems that can be associated with entrepreneurship. It is easy for entrepreneurs to have delusions of grandeur, to imagine that a market exists for a product when it does not, to use 'spin' to attract funds for investment and to resort to immoral or illegal measures when the money runs out. Christians should not imagine that they are impervious to such pressures or immune to serious temptations. Like everyone else, we need to be aware of economic realities. It is an abuse of our faith to turn to God for a quick fix when we have acted foolishly or dishonestly.

Entrepreneurs on the rise

Entrepreneurs now have a much more positive image than they did twenty-five years ago. Richard Branson himself deserves much credit for this. Throughout his career he has cultivated an open, informal and unconventional image which has connected well with the public. His appetite for record-breaking stunts could have led to his being seen as a maverick, but his business career has been solidly grounded in giving the customer value for money, whether that be with Virgin Records, Virgin Atlantic, Virgin Trains or Virgin Money. Branson has consistently shown astuteness and vision in spotting talent, identifying opportunities and securing the necessary resources to make his vision a reality. Branson is a great champion and promoter of entrepreneurship. Not only does he believe it is the best antidote to poverty; entrepreneurship is 'about turning what excites you in life into capital, so that you can do more with it and move forward with it'.

Another entrepreneur who made a hugely positive impact on the public was the founder of the Body Shop International, Anita Roddick. She opened the first Body Shop in Brighton in 1976, providing quality skincare products in refillable containers and sample sizes, marketed in a measured but very informative way without hype. The company rapidly assumed a stance of avoiding products tested on animals. Roddick travelled the world and discovered a wide range of 'natural' methods and ingredients for improving the quality of skin and health. Over thirty years the number of stores grew worldwide to 2,000. She developed the idea of corporate social responsibility long before it became commonplace, and advocated it in an authentic and wholehearted way. In 2006, a year before her death from a brain haemorrhage, she and her husband Gordon took the controversial decision to sell the Body Shop to the

French cosmetics giant L'Oréal for £652 million. She defended this on the grounds that she could do more long-term good by influencing the decisions of a huge company.

Along with other men and women of enterprise, Richard Branson and Anita Roddick contributed to a sea change in the way that entrepreneurs are viewed. Clearly there will always be some dodgy entrepreneurs. A fresh wave of them appeared in the dot.com phenomenon around the turn of the century. But at their best, entrepreneurs are now admired for four key qualities, all beginning with the letter 'i'.

Innovation: We have already highlighted this as a defining aspect of the entrepreneur. Innovation is not just about having a bright idea. As Bolton and Thompson rightly note, 'It is about seeing the creative new idea through to completion, to final application.' The discerning entrepreneur sees how to implement an idea.

Industriousness: Entrepreneurs are prepared to roll up their sleeves and work hard. This is especially the case in the early stages of a business. At a stage when they cannot employ many other people, entrepreneurs need to master a wide range of skills themselves. Success is as much about perspiration as inspiration.

Integrity: The entrepreneurs who command most respect display integrity. They live integrated lives that display honesty, consistency and transparency. This does not mean they avoid any sniff of controversy: that would be impossible in a world which abounds with moral complexity and where people's views vary greatly. But entrepreneurs with integrity are able to defend their actions in public with a minimum of embarrassment.

Inspiration: Entrepreneurs with these qualities have a contagious effect. They are an inspiration to others. They encourage others to follow in their footsteps and do likewise – not in a 'copycat' sort of way, but finding a distinctive niche where they make their mark and create a business.

Entrepreneurship today

The recession which followed the global financial crisis in 2006–8 had a positive effect in encouraging entrepreneurship. This is partly because many people lost their jobs, could not find alternatives, and so were forced back on their own resources to continue in work. It is also because many became disillusioned with the big corporate scene, launching out with their own business because they believe it represents a more satisfying way to earn a living.

No-one in the UK speaks with more enthusiasm and authority about entrepreneurship than Luke Johnson. He writes a weekly column on the virtues and challenges of entrepreneurship for *The Sunday Times*. He is the chair of StartUp Britain, the national campaign to stimulate start-up growth, and in 2013 he launched the Centre for Entrepreneurs, an independent non-profit think tank which promotes the role of entrepreneurs in society. Johnson has an impressive record as a serial entrepreneur. He led the growth of Pizza Express between 1993 and 1999, and he is part-owner of Patisserie Holdings, which has grown thirty-fold since he took control nine years ago.

Luke Johnson believes that a 'wave of entrepreneurialism' has driven business recovery in the UK. He points to the record number of business start-ups in recent years. Johnson claims:

There is one player in society who creates jobs, and it is not big companies. The majority of new jobs in this country were created by companies employing 50 people or fewer . . . There is a cultural shift going on in the UK towards self-employment. The numbers have suggested there are more than 4.5 million people working for themselves. It is a very exciting time.

Johnson thinks that starting a business is easier, quicker and cheaper than ever thanks to new technology. True, launching a business is not for the faint-hearted. 'You need to have high energy, you need to be confident, you need to have self-belief, and you need to have a capacity for hard work.' Capital need not be a barrier to entry, because many new businesses these days do not require much investment. The digital revolution has made it easier to test ideas and experiment, to see if an idea will work.

Johnson's verdict is clear: 'Entrepreneurs have higher profiles than in the past and are seen as role models.' Their image has changed out of all recognition from the prejudice encountered by Branson in the early 1970s.

Entrepreneurs and the church

How is the church responding to this entrepreneurial revolution? Does it show much awareness of what is going on? Has it embraced the more positive view of entrepreneurship we are seeing in today's society? The answer is both yes and no.

A book published just before the 2015 General Election, with the hope that it would influence public debate about key social issues, is *On Rock or Sand? Firm Foundations for Britain's Future*. It is edited by Archbishop John Sentamu and is a collection of essays covering such areas as the economy, poverty, education and healthcare, work, ageing, children and young people and the Welfare State. The contributors are impressively qualified, well-known names in different fields.

Sadly, the chapter on the way ahead for the British economy fails even to mention entrepreneurs. It offers worthy sentiments on the principles of sustainable growth, shared prosperity and responsible business practices, but fails to recognize the contribution that small-scale business can make or might already be making.

A different type of book with entrepreneurship at its very heart is *The Minister as Entrepreneur*, written by Michael Volland. This has an admirable aim: to contribute to the emergence of a culture in which entrepreneurs and entrepreneurship are properly understood and recognized as gifts of God to his church – especially in a time of rapid cultural change. Michael begins with the bold statement: 'I am a Christian minister. I am also an entrepreneur.' By this he means not an ability to make money but an attitude of relentlessly and energetically wanting to improve things. This is characteristic of many, like him, who advocate pioneer or 'fresh expressions' ministry, developing new forms of ministry to meet the challenge of an increasingly secular society.

Michael's book is influenced by Bolton and Thompson's *Entrepreneurs*. He adapts their definition of an entrepreneur to produce a more 'Christian' version: 'a visionary who, in partnership with God and others, challenges the status quo by energetically creating and innovating in order to shape something of kingdom value'. By 'kingdom value' Michael means the furtherance of God's coming kingdom of justice, provision, wholeness, peace and reconciliation. (We shall say more about the idea of building the kingdom in chapter 6.) Armed with this definition, he found eighteen parish priests in the Durham diocese who displayed entrepreneurial traits. At the time he worked at Cranmer Hall in Durham. He then focused on interviewing seven who achieved outstanding results in an online test for entrepreneurial characteristics. He found that these priests were not necessarily doing things that were strikingly new, but they had a positive 'glass half full' attitude which enabled them to see potential obstacles as challenges and opportunities.

Michael rapidly discovered that 'entrepreneur' is a contested term in the church. He invited thirty people engaged in various forms of Christian ministry to comment on the word 'entrepreneur'. While many respondents were positive, several reacted strongly against it or were decidedly ambivalent:

- 'I understand the reason why the term is used, but I struggle to feel entirely comfortable with it. It is difficult to detach the word "entrepreneur" from the world of business and commerce – which has sufficient connotations of consumerism and materialism to make it somewhat unhelpful.'
- 'I loathe the use of the word "entrepreneur". We do not need to borrow more terms from the market – our faith has been privatized enough as it is! The word entrepreneur has too many connotations with taking risks for personal gain. If one looks at contemporary understandings of the entrepreneur it is associated with such programmes as *The Apprentice* and *Dragons' Den*. These programmes reflect the ruthlessness of modern capitalist society, and are inherently confrontational and combative.'
- 'Entrepreneur is not a term I would use in relation to my own pioneering ministry. I would prefer to use a word like prophetic. I suppose my own role is entrepreneurial as I began more or less with a blank piece of paper and a time span in which to achieve something. But it is not a definition that sits comfortably with me.'

Volland makes a strong case for using the word entrepreneur in the remainder of the book, emphasizing especially the key qualities of vision, creativity and innovation in shaping something of kingdom value. But this mixed response that he encountered from church leaders shows that the word still carries some negative connotations. These comments also suggest a lingering suspicion of or hostility to business in certain church quarters – a tendency we know all too well.

We hope very much that discussion about 'entrepreneur' in church circles gets beyond the question of whether it is a useful metaphor for church pioneers. Entrepreneurs who work in business need to be welcomed for the essential work that they do. Many of them are making a major contribution to furthering the kingdom, through the provision of innovative goods and services, providing employment, witnessing to their business contacts and generally making the world a better place. Perhaps the church in the UK would appreciate entrepreneurs more if it woke up to what is going on in other parts of the world.

Entrepreneurs worldwide

Watching the news often feels like a tale of non-stop disaster. Wars, terrorism, earthquakes, famines, fires, floods, the refugee crisis, the warming of the atmosphere, the growth of intolerance – it sometimes feels as if all major global trends are veering in a negative direction.

However, hidden beneath and behind so much bad news, there is genuinely good news. It is often said, for instance, that 'the rich are getting richer and the poor are getting poorer', but this statement is only partially correct. It is true that the rich are, in general, becoming even richer – some would say obscenely rich. But the poor, in general (obviously there are exceptions), are not becoming poorer. One of the eight Millennium Development Goals was to halve the proportion of people in absolute poverty between 1990 and 2015, i.e. those whose income is less than $1.25 a day. The target was actually met five years early, in 2010. How was this achieved? Not in the main by charity, international aid or debt relief, though these all made modest contributions. People have been brought out of poverty by economic growth, notably in the 'BRIC' countries of Brazil, Russia, India and China, but also in many African countries. Most of this economic growth has been in the small- to medium-sized businesses sector. Entrepreneurial flair and initiative are playing a major part in changing the fortunes not just of individuals and families, but also of workforces and nations.

The Middle East remains a deeply troubled part of the world, beset by conflict and violence. It is the area where Christians are most thinly spread, suffering persecution from militant strands of Islam. But in the three great continents of Africa, Asia and South America, development proceeds apace. You do not have to look far to find positive news stories in Botswana, China or Chile. These are also the continents where – in contrast to the increasingly secularized West – the Christian church is growing fast. Christian faith is keenly embraced in many countries that received it through colonization by the civilization that has now largely abandoned it.

Pentecostalism and the prosperity gospel

Within the overall picture of gradual church expansion in the Global South, one form of Christianity is experiencing spectacular growth: Pentecostalism. We use this word broadly to include not just churches which call themselves Pentecostal, but others which display Pentecostal characteristics. These churches emphasize lively preaching of the Bible, fervent prayer, the baptism and gifts of the Holy Spirit, and charismatic worship. Current estimates are that 80% of Protestant growth worldwide is attributable to Pentecostalism.

Is there a connection between the high level of entrepreneurial activity in these countries and the type of Christianity that is popular? A growing body of scholarly opinion believes there is. Studies by Andy Henley, Peter Heslam and Shane Clifton all cite evidence that Pentecostal versions of Christianity are producing a higher-than-average level of entrepreneurial activity. This is because these Christians refuse to see themselves as victims, believing that through the power of the Holy Spirit – inspiring their own hard work – they can wrest themselves out of poverty. Their conviction is that, whatever the rights and wrongs of contemporary trading systems, they can succeed and prosper in and through those systems.

Pentecostalism in the Global South is often associated with the prosperity gospel. This is understandable, because many of the churches that teem with aspiring entrepreneurs teach this 'gospel' in some form. It is a type of teaching that arose in the USA after the Second World War, before becoming popular and spreading rapidly during the 1980s and 1990s.

What are its key tenets? In essence, that the normal Christian life includes good health and substantial wealth. Faithful Christians who work hard and pay their tithes can expect God to bless them with financial prosperity. The salvation that Christ brings is holistic; it covers the whole of our lives.

Prosperity preachers have some favourite texts. They include:

- God's promise to the Israelites on the verge of the Promised Land: 'But remember the LORD your God, for it is he who gives you power to get wealth, so that he may confirm his covenant that he swore to your ancestors, as he is doing today' (Deuteronomy 8:18);

- the prophet Malachi's exhortation: 'Bring the full tithe into the storehouse, so that there may be food in my house, and thus put me to the test, says the LORD of hosts; see if I will not open the windows of heaven for you and pour down for you an overflowing blessing' (Malachi 3:10);

- John's wish for his friend Gaius: 'Beloved, I pray that all may go well with you and that you may be in good health, just as it is well with your soul' (3 John 2).

What is a balanced verdict on prosperity theology? It contains some important half-truths. Material possessions are gifts from God, and he intends human beings to enjoy them. By living sensibly, working hard and showing enterprise, we shall often – in the providence of God – become prosperous. But there is no automatic guarantee of this. Adversity can strike anyone, and that includes faithful Christians. The prosperity preachers are highly selective in the passages they quote. Jesus said: 'If any want to become my followers, let them deny themselves and take up their cross and follow me' (Mark 8:34). He warned: 'It is easier for a camel to go through the eye of a needle than for someone who is rich to enter the kingdom of God' (Matthew 19:24). The biblical material on wealth is varied, complex and contains many caveats and warnings. In the Old Testament, rich people are expected to be generous, and the godly rich usually are. When the rich flaunt their wealth, they are roundly criticized.

In reading the Bible, it is important not to universalize particular verses and passages and imagine that they apply to everyone everywhere. One entrepreneur we interviewed, Phil, shared some wise words about this. He himself has experienced a business career with many highs and lows. He said:

> It's a real challenge to discern as a Christian entrepreneur what promises God gives you and what promises he doesn't. I read many promises in the Bible that God will look after us and be close to us. If I'm not careful I apply those promises and say God will always keep my business going, but I can't; even though God promises to look after me there is no promise that my business won't go bankrupt. The prosperity gospel goes clearly wrong because there are plenty of godly businessmen who undergo bankruptcy. It's a question of understanding – not taking the promises to be more than they are, nor taking the promises to be less than they are. It is very hard to balance.

We agree. Perhaps part of the answer lies in Ecclesiastes 3, which talks about a 'time' for everything. This includes a time for contrasting business activities: 'a time to plant, and a time to pluck up what is planted'; 'a time to throw away stones, and a time to gather stones together'; 'a time to tear, and a time to sew'. We need God's wisdom to discern which passages in the Bible apply specifically to us at any particular time.

The most worrying aspect about prosperity theology is the behaviour of those who are propagating it. Heslam acknowledges that 'the image of developing-world Pentecostal pastors . . . is of men in smart suits and flashy cars subsidized through the tithes of their slum-dwelling congregants'. It is church leaders who appear more prone to ostentatious living than the entrepreneurs whom they nurture.

A force for good

Heslam's studies of actual entrepreneurs in the Global South reveal many admirable men and women who are striving hard to reduce poverty, promote integrity and ensure sustainability. He has told the stories of some in his regular column in *Faith in Business Quarterly*. Running a business well, a business which does demonstrable good in society and serves to improve the quality of life, a business which brings pleasure to the God we serve, is a strong uniting thread across cultures and continents. We can identify with those whose hopes and aspirations we share. Entrepreneurs of the world unite!

4. 'NOT A MAN BUT A PURPOSE'

Christian entrepreneurs in the UK also have a rich heritage in this country to draw on. There are many fine examples of Christian entrepreneurship from the past.

Merchants and traders have abounded from time immemorial, but the notion of companies owned by individuals in which others might invest started to take root in the seventeenth century. In the UK, Christians from the Nonconformist churches (churches which had broken away from the Church of England) played a major part in this flowering of enterprise. This was partly because they were barred from other professions such as politics, the civil service, universities and the law, but it was also because they nurtured the qualities needed to succeed in business. They displayed many of the characteristics which the German sociologist Max Weber identified with the Protestant work ethic. They were hard working, disciplined, honest and prepared to forgo material pleasure in favour of long-term investment.

The Nonconformist group that has wielded the most influence in British business history is that of the Quakers, or Society of Friends. Founded in the mid-seventeenth century, they practised simple services of worship where they listened silently to God and then shared their experiences. Quaker leader George Fox had little respect for established authority; he advocated plain dress, plain speaking and a strict moral code.

Historian James Walvin believes the Quakers did well in business for a variety of reasons. He highlights the following:

- The Quakers' fierce commitment to *honesty*. Their yea was yea and their nay was nay (Matthew 5:37). They were accepted as honest even by those who disliked them. During the eighteenth century, this reputation made people ready to trust them to look after their money. Many of the early banks, including Lloyds and Barclays, were founded by Quakers. Honesty stood them in good stead in other areas of business too. Their word could be trusted, their goods were what they seemed, and their prices were both fixed and reasonable.

- The Quakers' system of *mutual accountability*. They kept checks on one another, and had to answer for their behaviour to their local meeting. It was considered shameful for a Quaker business to run into debt or go bankrupt. Prominent Quakers – even those who were competitors within the same industry – met regularly, passed on advice and warned one another against dubious prospects or dodgy traders.

- The Quakers' emphasis on *education*. This flowed from the Protestant habit of reading the Bible for oneself. They wanted to understand the world that God had made. They set up their own schools and established apprenticeships for their children. Sons were often sent to a Quaker associate to learn a trade before returning to run the family business. Some powerful dynasties took shape, notably the three generations of Abraham Darby, who developed the iron and steam industry in Coalbrookdale, Shropshire during the eighteenth century.

The nineteenth century

In 1851, according to the religious census, there were a mere 18,172 Quakers in the UK. Yet their commercial impact on the nation was out of all proportion to their numbers. As well as banking and engineering, they were prominent in confectionary, drinks, insurance, pharmaceuticals, railways, shoes, soap, steel and textiles. But other Nonconformist denominations were also prominent: Congregationalists, Methodists and, from the late nineteenth century, the Brethren.

Ian Bradley's *Enlightened Entrepreneurs* is an excellent introduction to those who were at the heart of this industrial revolution. He shows what these entrepreneurs shared in common. They all came from comparatively humble origins. They all grew their businesses by seizing on some new, relatively simple technique which brought spectacular results. They all cared deeply about their employees and believed they knew what was best for them – hence their reputation for being 'paternalist'. Although in due course they became wealthy, their lifestyles were restrained rather than extravagant. They enjoyed bracing physical exercise and most were teetotallers. They ended up giving much of their hard-earned wealth away, either in their lifetime or through generous endowment of trusts.

Bradley recounts detailed life stories of ten notable Victorian entrepreneurs. We shall confine ourselves to four case studies. These include two that feature in Bradley's book, those concerning Titus Salt and George Cadbury, and two other case studies worthy of attention: C. & J. Clark and John Laing (though Laing belongs to a later generation, most of his working life being in the twentieth century). We have made our choice not just because the lives of these individuals are particularly interesting, but because the story of what happened to their companies after they died is fascinatingly varied.

C. & J. Clark

Clarks the shoe retailer originated with two brothers, Cyrus and James. Several Nonconformist family firms were in fact run for a while by two brothers in tandem. Usually one of the brothers had a dominant influence. This was not the case with Cyrus and James, so it is appropriate that the initials of both live on in the company name.

Cyrus Clark, the elder brother, was a tanner who began by making sheepskin rugs in the small Somerset town of Street in 1825. One day his younger brother James had the idea of making slippers from the offcuts and cast-offs. They called the first sheepskin slippers they made in 1828 Brown Peters. Their unique design proved popular and by 1842 sales were averaging 1,000 pairs per month. The slippers were made by hand in Street. There were no factories, so the brothers relied on outworkers to meet the growing demand. The workers collected the leather from the tannery, with a pattern, took it home and turned it into slippers. Every Friday the finished footwear was taken to Cyrus and James and exchanged for wages. Business was so brisk that the Clark brothers won two awards at the 1851 Great Exhibition.

Crisis hit the company in 1863. A national recession had dire effects and the Clarks needed external financial support. Being Quakers, they followed the typical pattern of turning to contacts in the wider Quaker community. This support came with conditions: Cyrus and James were to step down and William, James's youngest son, who had displayed good business acumen, should take over. William duly modernized the manufacturing process by introducing a factory system and investing in Singer sewing machines – then a groundbreaking piece of technology. C. & J. Clark was revitalized, the loan to senior Quakers was repaid and the company moved forward with new developments like the Hygienic range. Launched in 1883, this was the first shoe designed to fit the shape of the foot, an innovation that is still the bedrock of Clarks' 'comfort' reputation. William also remained true to Quaker ideals, investing in the local community and building his workers homes, many of which survive in Street today.

The company continued to grow steadily during the early decades of the twentieth century. Women became major customers, and Clarks were happy to oblige the new trend to display female ankles. They introduced a choice of width fittings for children's shoes and made a foot-measuring gauge – two significant innovations. During the Second World War, when materials were scarce, they designed a unique, hinged wooden sole, enabling the company to carry on supplying Britain with shoes in difficult times.

The postwar period has been one of continuing growth. Clarks steadily acquired other shoe manufacturers such as K Shoes (1981). The company has twice seriously considered going public (in 1988 and 1993), but in each case drew back from the brink, deciding to remain a family-owned business. In the 1990s, rising costs led it to relocate manufacturing abroad. Clarks shoes are predominantly designed in the UK, but the shoes are now made in India, Brazil, Cambodia, China and Vietnam. Independent auditors as well as on-site teams monitor conditions to promote the best working practices. Clarks remains the leading shoe brand in Britain, and the fourth largest footwear company in the world. It is 84% owned by the Clark family.

Titus Salt

The splendidly named Titus Salt was a Congregationalist. His father Daniel was a Bradford wool-stapler. As a teenager, Titus learned to buy good fleeces at auction, assessing the wool according to the fibre's length, softness and fineness, and preparing it for spinning into yarn. He took over his father's firm in 1834.

Titus was constantly on the lookout for new materials and his breakthrough happened when he noticed a pile of 300 dirty-looking bales lying in a Liverpool warehouse. They turned out to be fleeces of the Peruvian alpaca. Impressed by the fleeces' straightness and length, he took a sample back to Bradford for experiment. He discovered it produced a high-quality yarn.

In 1837 Salt launched Alpaca Orleans, a fabric made from alpaca and cotton, which became a popular dress material for Victorian ladies – highlighted when Queen Victoria sent Salt the fleeces of the two alpaca she kept in Windsor Park to be made into cloth. Salt also introduced the use of mohair, another long-staple combing wool from the fleece of the angora goat in Turkey. Through developing these two unusual wools, Salt became the leading figure in the West Yorkshire worsted industry.

Salt grew rapidly in wealth, so that by 1844 he and his family were able to move to a large house ten miles outside

Bradford. Nevertheless, he remained a stickler for hard work and was at the mill by six o'clock every morning. He was also determined to do something about the conditions in which his workers lived. Mid-nineteenth-century Bradford had grown from a population of 43,000 in 1831 to 103,000 in 1851. It was a filthy, unhygienic city and appalling for children; average life expectancy was just eighteen years. Over 200 mill chimneys emitted sulphurous fumes. Salt fitted special smoke burners to the chimney stacks of his own five mills to reduce pollution. He gave Bradford a 61-acre park so that the public could enjoy some relatively fresh air. Then in 1850 he took the radical step of relocating his company from the city to a new greenfield site three miles north-west of Bradford, on the south bank of the River Aire. The village of Saltaire was born.

There Salt erected a new mill – the world's first totally integrated woollen textile factory. It stood six storeys high, with large plate-glass windows and flues making the building light and airy. At the mill's opening Salt said: 'I will do all I can to avoid evils so great resulting from polluted air and water, and hope to draw around me a well fed, contented and happy band of operatives.'

Then, over a twenty-year period, Salt constructed a village of 850 dwellings in twenty-two streets to accommodate all his 4,500 employees. The houses were solidly built and mostly terraced; they varied in size according to occupational status, but they were all distinct improvements on the cramped and squalid conditions of Bradford. A large Congregationalist church, public baths, school, hospital, library, sports field and institute followed, but no pub; a notice at the entrance to Saltaire said: 'Abandon beer all ye who enter here.' Salt had seen the evils of over-drinking and was a strict teetotaller. He was an unashamed paternalist, banning smoking, gambling and swearing in the village park, but his workers' health benefited from his concern for their welfare, just as their incomes did from the company's success.

Titus Salt was knighted in 1869. Five years later, an ornate statute of him was unveiled outside Bradford Town Hall. Salt responded with characteristic modesty and a dash of humour: 'So they want to make me into a pillar of salt!' His motto was *Quid non, Deo Juvante*, meaning 'What can we not do, with God's help?' It sums up his attitude to life. When he died in May 1876, an estimated 120,000 people turned out to pay their respects. This speaks volumes for the affection in which he was held.

Sadly, Salt's business survived less well than that of most of his distinguished Christian contemporaries. His sons took over the company, but it went bankrupt before being revived by a group of Bradford businessmen. Without regaining its former glory, Salt's mill continued through much of the twentieth century before closing down in 1985. Saltaire has become less of a working community and more of a tourist attraction. The mill now houses art galleries, restaurants, shops and small businesses.

George Cadbury

A curious irony pervaded the Quaker practice of business. They believed in plain dress and a simple lifestyle, and generally stayed true to these principles with regard to their own behaviour, but this did not stop them supporting the needs and wants of those who sported a more affluent lifestyle. Their shopkeepers sold a range of expensive clothes, frills and elaborate accessories. And nineteenth-century Quakerism will forever be linked with the production of chocolate – then a luxury item. Fry, Rowntree and Cadbury, the three great chocolate companies, were all Quaker family firms.

None of these companies sold chocolate bars to begin with. They all started as makers of hot drinks, notably cocoa and drinking chocolate. Quaker businessmen developed these drinks as an alternative to alcoholic beverages.

Richard and George Cadbury were sons of John Cadbury, who founded the business in the centre of Birmingham. True to the Quaker pattern, George was sent away at the age of seventeen to do a two-year apprenticeship with Joseph Rowntree in York. Both Rowntree's and Cadbury's then lagged well behind the Bristol firm Fry's in terms of sales and size. When George returned to Birmingham, he and Richard took over the firm from their father in 1861.

Their first four years as, effectively, joint managing directors were extremely difficult. They faced stiff competition and Cadbury's was making a loss. The brothers lived extremely frugal lives in their concern to save money. By 1865 the commercial prospects were so bleak that they considered closing the business.

Richard and George Cadbury were two contrasting characters. Richard had the sunnier disposition and was very popular with the workers. George had a more serious outlook; he was strategic and far sighted in his thinking. One colleague said of him, 'He was not a man but a purpose.' Despite their differences, the brothers complemented each other effectively.

In 1865 George took a major gamble. Cocoa was then a very impure substance. It was heavily adulterated with starches such as potato, flour and treacle to make the taste of the cocoa bean more palatable. The Cadburys heard of a Dutch manufacturer, Coenraad van Houten, who had developed a hydraulic press that extracted the cocoa fat and made the addition of other substances unnecessary. The result was a purer, smoother drink which tasted much more pleasant.

George visited Holland and, despite speaking no Dutch, managed to persuade van Houten to sell him a cocoa press. It was a remarkable achievement which saved the company and set it on the road to prosperity. Cadbury's became the first British company to produce pure cocoa. They were not shy about proclaiming this. Previous generations of Quaker businesspeople had refrained from advertising, but the Cadbury brothers took the plunge. Cadbury's Cocoa Essence was advertised in newspapers, on posters and even on London buses. Richard came up with the slogan 'Absolutely Pure, Therefore Best'. It worked. Richard was no mean artist and even drew pictures for some of the adverts himself, using his own children as models.

While the new cocoa drink was the foundation of their success, the Cadburys started to experiment with making chocolate bars. They mixed the extracted cocoa butter with sugar to make chocolates with cream and fruit-filled centres. The Fancy Box was launched.

Commercial success did not diminish the brothers' Christian zeal. George led a service at the start of each day: a passage of Scripture, followed by a time of silence for prayer and then the singing of a hymn. On Sundays he taught Scripture and basic literacy to working-class people at a Sunday school in central Birmingham. His experience 'among the back streets of Birmingham' led him to the conclusion 'that it is impossible to raise a nation morally, physically and spiritually in such surroundings, and that the only effective way is to bring men out of the cities into the country and to give to every man his garden where he can come in touch with nature and thus know more of nature's God'.

Like Salt, Cadbury decided to move the company out of the city. In 1878 he bought a 14-acre site south-west of Birmingham, Bournville. First he built a light and spacious factory, and then he built houses for his 320 workers. Unlike in Saltaire, the houses all had gardens; it was George's conviction that 'no man ought to be compelled to live where a rose cannot grow'.

The fortunes of the company were now set on a steadily ascending curve. However, its reputation came under threat in the 1900s when allegations spread that workers at the São Tomé plantation off Angola were effectively working as slaves. Cadbury's imported many of its cocoa beans from the island. George and his nephew William (Richard had died) were appalled and tried to investigate the rumours, but relied too much on the British government to put pressure on the Portuguese colonial government – which it was slow to do. In 1908 the London newspaper *The Standard* alleged that Cadbury's was profiting from slavery. The company sued the paper for libel. After a memorable court case, the jurors found in favour of Cadbury's, but the damages against *The Standard* amounted to a derisory farthing, suggesting they saw the case as less than clear cut. Soon afterwards, Cadbury's stopped using São Tomé and started importing cocoa from West Africa.

Although the slavery controversy was stressful, it does not seem to have seriously damaged the business in the eyes of the public. Cadbury's launched another long-term winner with the Dairy Milk chocolate bar in 1905. Over a period of fifty years their sales caught up with Fry's, who were much slower to innovate. In 1918 Cadbury's took over Fry's. George Cadbury died in 1922. His favourite quotation was, 'Whatsoever thy hand findeth to do, do it with [all] thy might' (Ecclesiastes 9:10 AV). He certainly followed that adage.

Cadbury's continued to grow as one of the world's great confectionery manufacturers throughout the twentieth century. In 1962, however, it took the fateful decision to become a public limited company. This attracted investors' capital, and in 1969 Cadbury's took over the drinks company Schweppes to form Cadbury Schweppes. But it also meant that Cadbury's became a target for other companies, culminating in a takeover by the American multinational Kraft Foods in 2008. This is a development that many both inside and outside the company lament. In her fascinating book *Chocolate Wars*, a history of the company, family member Deborah Cadbury quotes Sir Adrian Cadbury, one of the company's longest-serving chairmen: 'It is very easy for a larger firm effectively to destroy the *spirit* of the firm they take over.' Deborah ends by asking the poignant questions: 'Will Kraft act for the betterment of the world – not just the top management? Will it be a tangible force for good in our global village? It is difficult not to feel sceptical.'

John Laing

John William Laing lived a very long life. Born in 1879, he died at the age of ninety-nine in 1978. He left school and started work at the age of fourteen. His career began in the nineteenth century, but he deserves to be remembered as probably *the* outstanding Christian entrepreneur of the first half of the twentieth century.

Laing was the son of a Carlisle builder; he became a Christian aged seven, at the local Brethren assembly his parents attended. He was bright enough to go to university, but was keen to get involved in his father's business. As his biographer says, 'The boy's heart was in the excitement and practical challenge and the companionship of hard work that the business represented.' Nor did Laing want to rest on privileges that his father's position might have brought him. He spent three years as a teenager mixing with navvies and learning the skills of bricklayer and mason. This meant he was literally earthed in the trade he went on to manage.

Laing was not content just with ordinary house building. He set his eyes on civil engineering projects. In 1898 he and his father bid successfully for a new electricity power station in Carlisle. This was followed by construction of a reservoir at Overwater, a demanding project that the young man again successfully managed.

Success may have made Laing overconfident, because he ran into serious difficulties on his next major project, with Barrow Corporation. This was for construction of new sewers near the docks. Laing agreed to a contract which left the construction company dangerously exposed. Trial borings had shown a working surface of sound dry clay. However, the work was undertaken in unusually bad weather and the Corporation at the request of local landowners agreed (over the head of Laing) to an altered line of sewer. Laing encountered the notorious problem of running sand, accentuated by a high water table. Sir Josiah Walker Smith, borough engineer and surveyor, was decidedly unsympathetic to Laing's difficulties. He stood firm on the conditions and threatened penalty clauses. A legal dispute loomed.

John Laing was intensely worried. A young man of twenty-eight, he feared for the collapse of the family firm. At this crucial moment in his life, he went for a walk near Furness Abbey on the edge of Barrow. He prayed fervently to God and vowed that, if God would show him a way through his troubles, he would make God a partner in the business. Laing drafted a programme for his life, which said first that 'the centre of my life was to be God – God as seen in Jesus Christ', and second that 'I was going to enjoy life, and help others to enjoy it'. On a sheet of hotel notepaper he set out a promise of how he would dispose of his income:

If income £400 p.a. give £50, live on £150, save £200

If income £4,000 p.a. give £1,500, live on £500, save 2,000.

God kept his side of the bargain. Helped by an able lawyer and supportive bank manager, Laing escaped from this hazardous project with the company intact. He made no profit on it, but he avoided serious losses. Laing did the necessary remedial work and was complimented on his integrity in court by the Official Referee. The incident left him with a residual prejudice against 'working in water'.

This formative experience probably confirmed Laing's desire 'to be the top contractor in the country'. He was motivated neither by money nor by power, but more by the challenge to be the best he possibly could be under God. It is no coincidence that Laing was a keen mountain climber. Mountains are there to be climbed. Construction projects are there to be won and completed.

Laing's expertise lay in precise and accurate costing of projects. He also showed sound strategic judgment in anticipating social and political needs. He developed Easiform, a method of building houses using concrete rather than bricks. This was ideal for the large-scale housing construction that was needed following both the First and Second World Wars, when skilled bricklayers were in short supply. In both wars he won numerous contracts connected with the military – munitions factories, army camps and airfields.

Laing understood the men who worked in construction. There are numerous stories about the way he interacted with them. Some stories reveal his tough side – he could be quick to reprimand people for sloppy work or to sack them for lack of punctuality. Others show his humanity and compassion – when employees found themselves in difficult circumstances he would grant them time off or provide financial support.

He was one of the first employers in the industry to introduce a Holidays-with-Pay scheme.

By 1920 Laing had his eyes set on running a national construction company. He moved the company's head office from Carlisle to London, situated at Mill Hill. Laing and his wife Beatrice bought an attractive house nearby, where they loved to offer hospitality.

Laing was careful with his money, but also extremely generous, and gave away large sums to many Christian causes, often anonymously. He was always an active member of the local Brethren church, and this was his first loyalty, but his outlook was very much that of the 'open' rather than 'closed' Brethren. He supported many evangelical causes of a non-denominational character. Although a man of simple faith, he appreciated the need to defend and promote it intellectually; his money lay behind the foundation both of London Bible College and Tyndale House, a centre for evangelical research scholarship in Cambridge. In the 1950s, the commission to build the new Coventry Cathedral gave him huge pleasure.

Laing was knighted in 1959, as were his two sons Kirby and Maurice, who followed him at the company's helm, in the 1960s. When he died in 1978, the fellow elder at his church, F. M. Hudson, gave a very apt address in which he singled out Laing's qualities from the initials of his name: Loyalty, Authority, Industry, Naivety (meaning artless simplicity) and Generosity. The latter quality was illustrated by the fact that, after his death, his net estate was revealed to be a mere £371. Laing had proved true to the promise made to God at Furness Abbey and given almost all his wealth away.

Under Martin Laing, John's grandson, the company's activities spread to many other countries. Then came the 1990s, a difficult decade. Hit by the recession, the company faced falling profits due to overcapacity in the sector and serious cost overruns on the Millennium Stadium project in Cardiff. In 2001 the momentous decision to sell the construction division to O'Rourke was taken. Since then Laing has changed character. It has become a property developer, financing infrastructure projects such as roads, railways, hospitals and schools through Public–Private Partnerships and Private Finance Initiatives.

Post-mortem

Anyone who founds a successful company has a choice about how to pass it on. Do they sell it to the employees, to an investor, to another company, or keep it in the family? These stories illustrate the variety of options, and the fact that what then happens to a company is hard to predict. Of the four companies we have examined, one, Clarks, has continued with its core business relatively unscathed; another, Salt, has disappeared altogether; a third, Cadbury, remains a distinctive brand but within a large conglomerate which appears not to share its original ethos; while a fourth, Laing, now operates in a different sector but one related to its past.

This diversity of outcome may make us wonder how worthwhile being an entrepreneur is. We may be tempted to share the despair of Ecclesiastes 2:18: 'I hated all my toil in which I had toiled under the sun, seeing that I must leave it to those who come after me – and who knows whether they will be wise or foolish?' Yet things can be worth doing in their own time even if they do not last indefinitely. The ebb and flow of companies has its place in God's purposes. The same might be said of these Christian entrepreneurs as was said of King David, who, 'after he had served the purpose of God in his own generation, died' (Acts 13:36). Cyrus and James Clark,

Sir Titus Salt, George Cadbury and Sir John Laing – along with many others – all did a great deal of good in their lifetimes. We can be inspired by the high standards of business ethics that they practised; by their shrewd and successful innovations; by the humane and caring treatment of their workforces; by the faith that so strongly motivated them; and by the generosity with which they gave their money away. Yes, Christian entrepreneurs in the UK have a very noble heritage.

5. COMMERCIALIZING INNOVATION

We have set entrepreneurship in a biblical, national, international and historical context. We now turn to the main theme of the book, which we introduced in the first chapter: the interviews carried out with fifty Christian entrepreneurs.

In chapter 3 we mentioned the growing numbers of entrepreneurs in the UK. Starting your own business has become very popular. You may wonder whether this growth is reflected in the church. Are there more or fewer Christians than average among this expanding band of entrepreneurs? Are Christians wielding an unusual amount of influence, as was clearly the case among Nonconformists in the nineteenth century?

We must confess that we do not know the answer to that question. To be able to answer it with confidence would necessitate a major national survey. Nevertheless, from the research that we have undertaken, we can report a strong sense that the spirit of entrepreneurship is alive and well in the Christian community.

In March 2009, when the UK was in recession following the global financial crisis, Faith in Business held a well-attended conference on entrepreneurship. Most of the participants were involved in entrepreneurial activity of some sort. They seemed undeterred by the traumatic events of the previous two years. Their faith in God gave them a confidence that it was still worth investing in exciting new ideas. Banks may have been lending less, but entrepreneurs have ways of finding the investment finance they need, and for small-scale ventures, family and friends often provide the initial outlay. The conference underlined the fact that entrepreneurship is an ongoing social necessity, even – indeed especially – during an economic downturn. Delegates gained encouragement from meeting kindred spirits and drew inspiration from the God who gives us our creative juices.

Kina's research

With this existing interest in entrepreneurship, Faith in Business was happy to support Kina when she made her proposal to interview fifty entrepreneurs. We already had a solid pool of entrepreneurs with whom we were in touch. About twenty of these fifty entrepreneurs were existing contacts – people who have attended Faith in Business events, have spoken at these events, or with whom Richard has had a long-standing relationship.

However, we also wanted to branch out and make new contacts, so we set about finding more entrepreneurs. This did not prove difficult. Suggestions came from a wide variety of sources. One contact put us on to another. A particularly helpful suggestion came from Peter Forster, Bishop of Chester. He mentioned Mark Mitchell, a leading layman in his diocese, whose story we told in chapter 1. Not only did

Mark prove fascinating in his own right; he also introduced Kina to a strong network of Christian entrepreneurs in northwest England. So eight further interviewees were friends of Mark's, involved in a variety of business sectors. We could have interviewed many more than fifty, and apologize to anyone we were not able to fit in who would have liked to be included. The line had to be drawn somewhere! We feel that fifty is a good number in that it amounts to a statistically significant sample. We have been able to identify trends and patterns.

We are aware that our pool of entrepreneurs does not include some high-profile Christian entrepreneurs. We think, for instance, of Brian Souter of Stagecoach, Camilla Stephens of Higgidy Pies and Julian Richer of Richer Sounds. Not everybody accepted the invitation to take part in the research, though the vast majority did. In any case, we have not confined ourselves to the well known. As we said in chapter 1, we wanted to research entrepreneurs at all stages of their careers: those who have recently started out as well as those who are well established.

The people we interviewed certainly work in a wide range of businesses. They include architecture, cars, ceramics, construction, consultancy, engineering, fashion, finance, food and drink, hospitality, law, media, product design, property, recycling, retail and social enterprise. The age range of our interviewees spanned at least fifty years, from mid-twenties to upper-seventies. A clear majority were white males, but we also interviewed several female entrepreneurs and a few from ethnic minorities.

If our sample was unrepresentative in one respect, it is that slightly more than half attended Anglican churches. This reflects the fact that Faith in Business is based in an Anglican theological college and many of our contacts are in the

Church of England. Our experience indicates that there are now plenty of entrepreneurs in the established church, more so than in the nineteenth century when Nonconformists dominated. Nonetheless, we suspect that Christian entrepreneurs are most numerous in the newer independent churches, which often have a charismatic or Pentecostal flavour. A few of our sample were from this background. However, our entrepreneurs tended not to express strong denominational allegiances. They went to church where they felt led or believed God had put them. They were Christians first and foremost and the fact that they attended an Anglican, Baptist or Catholic church (to name but three) was a secondary matter.

Entrepreneur defined

It is time to say more about our understanding of the word 'entrepreneur'. There is in fact a surprising lack of agreement about how it should be defined. At the most basic level, entrepreneur is often used simply of someone who starts up their own business. Leading columnist Luke Johnson appears to use the word in this simple sense.

Turning to more academic views of entrepreneurship, we find that different definitions abound. A French word, it is thought to have originated with the economist Richard Cantillon (1680–1734). Entrepreneur literally means someone who takes (*preneur*) between (*entre*). This would suggest a merchant who acts as a go-between in the trading process. A later French economist, Jean-Baptiste Say (1767–1832), went further by calling an entrepreneur one who undertakes an enterprise, typically a contractor who acts as intermediary between capital and labour. He emphasized the vital roles of an entrepreneur in forecasting, project appraising and risk-taking. In the early twentieth century the Austrian economist Joseph Schumpeter (1883–1950) was the shrewdest student and most prominent advocate of entrepreneurship. He highlighted the role of entrepreneurs as innovators: they devised new products and methods of production, often using new technology; some created new forms of organization and even conjured up new markets. Because this involved a threat to old, established ways of doing things, entrepreneurs brought with them an element of *creative destruction*.

In *Entrepreneurs*, Bolton and Thompson propose this definition: 'A person who habitually creates and innovates to build something of recognized value around perceived opportunities.' This definition identifies some key characteristics about entrepreneurs and has been quite influential; Michael Volland uses it as a starting point for his definition of a Christian minister as an entrepreneur. We believe it is less than comprehensive, however, and would like to suggest an alternative, building on the ideas of Canadian entrepreneurship expert Rick Goossen.

Our definition is: 'An entrepreneur pursues opportunities to commercialize innovation, taking the lead in marshalling resources and providing goods or services in the marketplace in a new and different way.' Each phrase requires some unpacking.

Pursues opportunities: Entrepreneurs are opportunistic. They see opportunities and go for them or exploit them. An astute entrepreneur resembles a striker with an eye for goal, seeing a space, darting into it and then finding the corner of the net.

Commercialize innovation: Entrepreneurs are not to be confused with inventors, who come up with clever ideas.

Entrepreneurs see how the idea can be put into effect and they can make money out of it. They have profit in view even if they are motivated by other factors in addition.

Taking the lead: Entrepreneurs are leaders. This does not necessarily mean they are at the head of an organization, though usually they will be. They grasp the initiative. An entrepreneur shares a vision and inspires others to follow.

Marshalling resources: Entrepreneurs identify what resources are needed and then set about gathering them together. Resources include capital, materials and people with the necessary skills. The word 'marshal' has connotations of bringing together, directing and aligning.

Providing goods or services in the marketplace: This essentially is what business is all about. A business provides goods, a service, and possibly both. Goods and services are bought and sold in a marketplace. Traditionally, this was a town-centre square. Today it takes many different forms, including the internet: eBay is a marketplace!

In a new and different way: This emphasizes the aspect of novelty. It is already present in the word 'innovation', but we stress it because this distinguishes entrepreneurs from many other businesspeople. They are doing or offering something not previously done by others.

In selecting our fifty interviewees, then, we had this working definition of entrepreneur in mind. We were looking for more than people who ran their own business, though that was our starting point. However, we do not pretend that all fifty fitted this definition fully. Some were stronger on some aspects of the definition than others, but all the key ingredients were there to a greater or lesser extent.

We need to say more about one particular kind of entrepreneur who has come to the fore in recent years: social entrepreneurs. Five interviewees were working in the area of social enterprise. One, Martin Clark, has even written a book about it: *The Social Entrepreneur Revolution*. Martin sees a social entrepreneur as 'somebody who tries to use entrepreneurship or business thinking to tackle a social problem or to meet a social need'. A social enterprise is a cross between a commercial business and a charity. The enterprise is looking for customers rather than donors and seeks to make a profit, but its main motivation is helping a particular group of people.

This is an important area of enterprise, and the numbers of social entrepreneurs have increased markedly in recent years, with Christians prominent among them. Yet we are wary of making too clear cut a distinction between social enterprise and many other areas of business. Most of the entrepreneurs we interviewed saw themselves as making a major contribution to society. As will become clear in later chapters, they are motivated by much more than money. They want to do good.

The questionnaire

We were particularly keen to investigate entrepreneurs' motivation, so many of Kina's questions focused on that. We wanted to discover what were the key characteristics that drove the practice of entrepreneurs and how these were related to the practitioners' faith. The questions also touched on other areas, such as the ethics of entrepreneurship and the relationship between the church and the entrepreneur.

We came up with twenty-three questions which were divided into three parts. The first, entitled 'Made in God's Image', covered such questions as 'What characterizes you as a *Christian* entrepreneur?', 'What gets you up in the morning?', 'What personal characteristics or behaviours do you demonstrate that contribute to success in your business life?' and 'Do you see yourself as a risk-taker?'

The second part, on 'The Practice of Entrepreneurship', included the questions 'Do you see yourself as having a calling?', 'Do you see yourself as contributing to the advance of God's kingdom?' and 'What were your most satisfying and humiliating moments in business?' It covered challenges to faith, 'dodgy' practices that constituted temptation, and the significance of prayer and Bible passages in people's lives.

The third part, on 'The Church and the Entrepreneur', looked at the attitude of the church towards what entrepreneurs do, as well as the topics of money, business and investment more generally.

In practice Kina did not stick rigidly to her prepared questions. Sometimes the answers that interviewees gave led naturally to follow-up questions. Occasionally time ran out so one or two questions remained unanswered. Most of the interviews took place at the entrepreneur's place of work, which helped set the business in context and added to our understanding.

In retrospect there are other questions we might usefully have asked. These include the size of the business (turnover, sales and number of employees) and the entrepreneur's practice of giving. But often such information surfaced in the course of the interview anyway. In some cases we asked supplementary questions by email or over the phone.

We believe that these interviews comprise a rich feast of fascinating material. In chapters 6–14 we shall draw selectively on our fifty interviews, as we consider the entrepreneurs' answers to the questions. We have grouped the material under twin themes occupying each chapter, e.g. vision and passion, or perseverance and hope. These themes emerged from the content of the interviews. They are the topics that kept coming to the fore as the entrepreneurs talked to us.

6. SEEKING FIRST GOD'S KINGDOM

Two questions we asked our interviewees had a particular theological slant. They concerned *calling* and *kingdom*.

'Calling' refers to the idea that God calls people to particular jobs, occupations or professions. In church history it has often been reserved for those who have embarked on so-called 'full-time Christian service': typically missionary, monk, nun, priest or minister. 'Calling' and 'vocation' are still words used most often in relation to ordained ministry. However, since the Reformation a current of thought has insisted that God calls people to all types of work. In the sixteenth century Martin Luther's revolutionary understanding of 'calling' broke the medieval mould. Luther emphasized the great variety of occupations in which it is possible to please God by hard work. The mother suckling her baby, the maid wielding her brush, the magistrate passing sentence and the merchant practising fair and honest trade were all doing something of real value if they performed these tasks in response to God's command and to his glory. This understanding was prominent in the English Puritan tradition. William Perkins said calling was 'a certain kind of life imposed on man by God for the common good'. But it usually involves more than the idea of embracing work as one's duty. American writer Os Guinness describes calling as 'the truth that God calls us to himself so decisively that everything we are, everything we do, and everything we have is invested with a special devotion and dynamism lived out as a response to his summons and service'. Those who feel called know that 'special devotion and dynamism' deep within them.

Given the diversity of the church's teaching on this subject, it is not surprising that our question 'Do you see yourself as having a calling to be an entrepreneur?' provoked different answers. This also reflected the diversity of people's experience. We wonder how you might respond to the question: 'Do you see yourself as having been called by God to be an entrepreneur?'

Calling – three responses

The majority of the interviewees felt that God had called them to be entrepreneurs. These were some of their replies:

- 'Yes, absolutely. More and more as I go on.'
- 'Yes, I was always engrossed in the business. I knew what I was doing was meant for me. It came from the everlasting Lord.'
- 'Yes, I have always thought this is my calling. God has given me particular passions, put me in the business and allows me to pursue them.'
- 'Yes, I feel I'm the one called to be an entrepreneur within our business, to make things happen. I have a calling to love people, to love God and to make God known.'

Two individuals who both studied law affirmed the idea of calling, though their careers had developed in very different directions:

- 'Without doubt. I read law at university but I would have been a lousy lawyer. I got into business in my mid-twenties and that's where I've felt at home.'
- 'Very much so. In a deep sense I feel called by God to do what I'm doing. Our firm's mission statement is expressed in terms of a call. We are called to be great lawyers, serving together.'

A second group of interviewees were more hesitant about the notion of calling. Some had founded a business without much sense of being an entrepreneur. Life in the corporate sector had not worked out for them – they had lost their job or become alienated from their company – and starting a business either seemed the only way to make a living or appeared much more congenial than their previous experience. Others felt a call to business; being an entrepreneur was a secondary matter. Most notably, for this second group a calling to entrepreneurship had developed over a period of time:

- 'I would say so now but not eighteen years ago. God's given me the opportunities, I've stepped into each opportunity and learned that I am an entrepreneur.'
- 'I didn't when I started the business. It's a story of different things fitting into place to where we are now. I call it *positioning* – into a place and time, then recognizing that's why God has put you there.'
- 'Originally I would say no. But now I do feel a calling, to create a strong company with a good product, and bring in the type of talent that will let the company

carry on. My calling has been to keep it going and make it strong.'

- 'Yes, but I didn't always. I came to realize that the things that made me excited, like winning new contracts or developing products, were part of how God has made me.'

These experiences illustrate the insight of the Danish philosopher and theologian Søren Kierkegaard: 'Life can only be understood backwards, but it must be lived forwards.' One entrepreneur, Adair, said as much: 'I kind of fell into being an entrepreneur. I learned that it was an expression of the way God has made me. It makes sense in retrospect.'

A third group, a small but significant minority, were totally resistant to the idea of calling. Some preferred the notion of doing God's will:

- 'My sense of calling is one of duty, and doing something good and useful.'
- 'I don't think God calls people. We can easily be deluded about what he's calling us to. The important thing is to discern and do God's will for us.'

Gary Grant felt the word was inappropriate in his case because he was an entrepreneur before he became a Christian; it was his decision rather than God calling that led him to set up The Entertainer. He said: 'What happened when I became a Christian was that I reviewed the way I was running the business. I felt I had the skills and talents for it, so it seemed right to remain an entrepreneur. God hasn't called me out of doing what I am doing.'

Ceramicist John Lovatt has a more theological objection: 'No, I was given the talent to be an entrepreneur, but not

called to it. I believe the term "calling" refers to the call to
follow Christ in all that I think or do, not necessarily a particular career, such as entrepreneurship. Nowadays, careers
can change part way through life, so Martin Luther's idea of
calling to a career for life is outdated.'

A biblical view

How should we respond to these objections?

It is true that the primary meaning of the word 'calling' in
the New Testament is the call to follow Jesus Christ. Jesus
called the fishermen James and John from their nets to follow
him (Mark 1:19–20). When challenged by the scribes and
Pharisees about his habit of eating with disreputable people,
he replied: 'I have come to call not the righteous but sinners'
(Mark 2:15–17). Paul says of the Christians at Rome that they
'are called to belong to Jesus Christ' (Romans 1:6). The Greek
word for 'church' is *ecclesia*, which literally means 'called out
ones'.

The question, then, is whether God also calls us to particular occupations. Paul certainly thought he was called to
be an apostle (Romans 1:1; 1 Corinthians 1:1), but it is difficult
to find New Testament passages that speak unambiguously
of calling in an everyday working context. The closest is
1 Corinthians 7:17–24, a passage which loomed large in
Luther's understanding. There Paul speaks of 'calling' with
regard to the 'place in life' or 'station' (slave or free; married
or single) that we occupy. 1 Corinthians 7:20 reads literally:
'Let everyone abide in the same calling wherein he was called'
(in the NRSV, 'Let each of you remain in the condition in which
you were called'). As John Lovatt points out, that can lead to
a rather static view of career, where one feels obliged to stay
in the same job indefinitely. When taken in the context of

wider biblical teaching, it need not be interpreted so woodenly. Paul himself did not stay in the same place for very long, except when he had no choice because he was imprisoned. One of the entrepreneurs we interviewed, Jerry Marshall, is a serial entrepreneur: he has started many different initiatives in his career and moved on quite quickly from one to another.

We believe that the word 'calling' rings true in many people's experience, and that it can provide a real source of strength amidst the ups and downs of entrepreneurial life. Feeling called to be an entrepreneur, or at least to running a particular business, can buttress the steel of character that is necessary when the going gets tough. One aspect of their role that all our entrepreneurs hated was telling employees that their jobs were redundant. Yet there are times when – for the sake of the company's survival – this needs to be done. Someone has to be the harbinger of bad news. For Christians who are seeking to discharge responsibilities like this as faithfully, sensitively and truthfully as they can, the conviction that God has *called* them may play an important part in steadying the nerves and carrying them through. You may have experienced this yourself.

However, we do not wish to insist on an understanding of calling where it does not really resonate with people's experience. For some, 'calling' has connotations of an audible voice – God speaking directly and unmistakably – and that is not how he seems to communicate with them. More fundamental (and this came strongly through the interviews as a whole) are these three pointers to becoming an entrepreneur:

Guidance: A strong sense that God has guided us to the type of work we are doing. The guidance may come from passages of Scripture, the advice of family and friends, time spent in prayer, or a deeply felt personal conviction.

Gifting: There needs to be a match between the entrepreneurial task and the skills and talents that we possess. Where a sense of calling is unaccompanied by any evidence of the necessary attributes – attributes listed in some detail in this book – individuals should ask themselves whether they have seriously misunderstood God's purposes for them.

Passion: We shall look at this in chapter 7. Entrepreneurs are usually passionate people. There is a product or service that they are desperately keen to deliver. Do you have a deep *enthusiasm* about something? Take heart from the fact that the word 'enthusiasm' means, literally, being indwelt or possessed by God. The Spirit of God can give us an energy that will have quite extraordinary outcomes.

Taken together, guidance, gifting and passion constitute a person who is hard to distinguish from one who feels called.

Jesus and the kingdom

Our question about calling was followed by one about kingdom. 'Do you see your work in business as contributing to the advance of God's kingdom?' The response to this was different. The answer here was a resounding *yes*. Our entrepreneurs felt that they *were* contributing to the advance of God's kingdom. However, answers to the follow-up question – 'If so, how?' – varied hugely. This begged the question of whether there was a shared understanding of what God's kingdom means.

If there is, as we suspect, a diverse understanding, this is not surprising. The kingdom of God is the dominating idea in the teaching and ministry of Jesus, certainly in the three Synoptic Gospels: Matthew, Mark and Luke. It is the nearest he comes to a company strapline. But Jesus never defines the kingdom. He says what it is *like* rather than what it is. His favourite device when preaching about the kingdom is to tell a parable, and if we analyse the many parables that begin 'the kingdom of God is like . . .', we discover a fascinating variety of themes. (We include here parables about the 'kingdom of heaven', Matthew's preferred terminology.) Take these nine themes from ten parables:

- surprise (Mark 4:26–29; the seed growing secretly)
- growth (Mark 4:30–32; the mustard seed)
- slowness to judge (Matthew 13:24–30; the wheat and the tares)
- penetration (Matthew 13:33; the leaven)
- value (Matthew 13:44–45; the treasure in the field, and the pearl of great price)
- forgiveness (Matthew 18:21–35; the unmerciful servant)
- generosity (Matthew 20:1–16; the labourers in the vineyard)
- festivity (Matthew 22:1–14; the wedding feast)
- preparation (Matthew 25:13; the wise and foolish virgins).

Other sayings of Jesus about the kingdom emphasize:

- perseverance (Luke 9:62: 'No one who puts a hand to the plough and looks back is fit for the kingdom of God')
- overthrow of evil (Luke 11:20: 'If it is by the finger of God that I cast out the demons, then the kingdom of God has come to you')
- repentance leading to salvation (Matthew 21:31: 'the tax collectors and the prostitutes are going in to the kingdom of God ahead of you').

As we assemble the different strands of Jesus' teaching about the kingdom of God, it becomes clear that God's kingdom is where God *reigns* or *rules*. It denotes territory where God's rule is acknowledged, where people accept his rule over the whole of their lives. It involves understanding what God is really like and living in a god-like way ourselves. There are many different aspects to this way of life.

The kingdom of God resembles a jigsaw with many pieces that fit together. Our fifty Christian entrepreneurs were attracted to different bits of the jigsaw. In analysing the answers to our question about the kingdom, four main responses emerged. Which of these do you identify with most closely?

Making the world a better place

First, there are entrepreneurs who believe they are contributing to God's kingdom by providing an excellent product or service. They are making the world a better place. They are enhancing the quality of people's lives, in line with God's purpose for his world.

David Ball is a good example. He believes that he has raised standards in the cement industry. To follow high standards is 'like saying I live my life by the Ten Commandments'. His latest innovative product, Cemfree, is making the world a better place because it drastically reduces carbon dioxide emissions.

Mike Clargo is a consultant who has launched a company called Inspirometer. This offers a metric device which helps people to measure swiftly and evaluate effectively the value of the meetings in which they are involved. Mike believes that improving the quality of meetings is crucial to the health of corporate relationships. Attending to this will not only make businesses more successful: 'More importantly, it will create a focus on what's important to God, to love, care and serve one another within organizations. It will make the God-shaped hole inside people more God-shaped.' Mike sees Inspirometer as kingdom work.

The view that their work is contributing to God's kingdom by making the world a better place was most clearly expressed by social entrepreneurs involved in the Global South. Natasha Rufus Isaacs comes from an aristocratic background and is a friend of the Duke and Duchess of Cambridge. In 2009 she and her friend Lavinia visited India and met women who were victims of sex-trafficking. 'God stirred our hearts,' says Natasha. They longed to set up a business that would provide the women with alternative employment.

The result of this heart-stirring was the founding of Beulah, a company which employs Indian women who have been victims of human trafficking to make luxury fashion items for a Western market. The name Beulah comes from Isaiah 62:4, a prophecy to the Jewish people in exile: 'You shall no more be termed Forsaken, and your land shall no more be termed Desolate; but you shall be called My Delight Is in Her, and your land Married [Beulah].' It appealed to Natasha and Lavinia because they were offering an alternative, positive destiny for the women they were helping. Alongside making up canvas bags, they do block-printing on the silks in Beulah's ready-to-wear collections.

Beulah sells dresses, jackets, skirts, trousers and scarves, but is best known for its signature all-silk dresses. Natasha's vision is one of reaching women in both West and East. On the one hand, they aim to empower women in India by giving them dignified paid employment. On the other hand, they aim to 'help rich women in this country who buy our dresses. They are just as lost sometimes, maybe not materially but spiritually. Our vision is to create a space where women feel beautiful inside and out, and then somehow experience the love of God.' By offering an ethical fashion store, Natasha and Lavinia seek to open the eyes of rich Western women to the good they can bring to the lives of women much poorer and less privileged than themselves.

Natasha's answer to the kingdom question was an unequivocal *yes*. She sees the work of Beulah both in empowering abused women in India and raising the consciousness of rich women in the West as advancing God's kingdom. 'Creating a space where women feel beautiful inside and out' is absolutely consistent with the ministry of Jesus, who did so much to raise the esteem of marginalized women he encountered.

Grant Smith works for Hand in Hand, a group of companies that has grown out of a charity of the same name, seeking to support poor people in Kenya. Grant is a quantity surveyor by background. Raising funds for educating poor children in the slums of Nairobi led Grant and his fellow trustees to ask: can we take this a step further? 'The logic of the business is that we create sustainable jobs that are properly paid and have a training programme of apprenticeships within the construction industry,' Grant says. 'The beauty of construction is that it provides an outlet for any academic ability that you have.' So Hand in Hand supports children with higher academic ability to become architects, engineers and quantity surveyors. If they have moderate academic ability they become carpenters, plumbers and electricians. If they have little academic ability they can still work on the construction site.

Hand in Hand has formed joint venture companies with business partners in the country, managed and operated by Kenyans. The group is active in the areas of commercial construction, residential construction and farming. Grant sees the advancement of God's kingdom in the development of local people so that they can run self-sustaining companies and become less dependent on the charitable side of Hand in Hand's work.

Andrew Tanswell has dedicated the past few years to bringing solar-powered products to the people of East Africa, first with ToughStuff and now with PoaPower. Andrew believes that this work is serving God's kingdom.

> There are 800 million people in sub-Saharan Africa with no access to electricity. If we can now provide power into homes that enables smart devices like phones to be powered, this enables the children to have online education in their own language to an educational standard tailored to the individual. There are all sorts of health benefits. People who live in the middle of nowhere can take a photo of their own eye so that an optician can then diagnose what prescription they might need.

How does this relate to God's kingdom? Andrew says: 'God wants us all to have life in all its fullness. I have life in abundance. A lovely family, a home, and lots of blessings. I want to see those blessings shared more widely.' PoaPower furthers God's kingdom by improving the quality of life of African people. By using energy from the sun it also provides electricity in an environmentally friendly way, liberating customers from the use of kerosene lamps that are both dangerous and polluting to the atmosphere.

Embodying Christian values

A second group of entrepreneurs saw advancement of the kingdom in terms of embodying Christian values. The emphasis here is less on the content of what is produced and more on the way the company is run and how it 'feels' to work there. Val King sees the creation of 'a very positive community' in her company, Rooflight, as fundamental to her motivation. We have already identified the values Rooflight lives by in chapter 1: integrity, care, empowerment and unity. All have a Christian basis.

Gordon Haynes works in the clothing import industry. His answer to the kingdom question was:

> I certainly hope so. I believe we are able to demonstrate Christian values in our business, even though the majority of people who work here aren't Christians. Our customers know that there are certain values we adhere to. They know we can be trusted. Most know that I am a Christian; certainly all our employees know I am and apply certain values within the business.

One distinguishing mark of his business is the absence of swearing. Gordon says: 'This is not because I imposed a no swearing rule, it just doesn't happen.'

Adair Richards, who runs a training company, answered the question similarly.

> When I train people I am imparting to them the wisdom that God has given me. That could be something like project management, which doesn't sound particularly Christian but it's very godly. It's important that projects are run efficiently, run well and run to time. When I work in the training room environment, I try really hard to value and give value to every person I am working with, so that it builds up their character, their identity, and shows them God's love. Even if it's the fact that I am collecting the coffee cups . . .

Adair is seeking to live out Jesus' servant style of leadership.

Andrew Perry and his wife ran a business which manufactured cakes and sold them into coffee shops and other outlets. It continues as COOK, which makes 'remarkable' food for your freezer. Andrew's understanding of the kingdom of God is that it expresses God's concern for the well-being of all people, especially the socially marginalized. His first four employees were rehabilitating drug addicts. COOK now employs ex-prisoners who are seeking to find new purpose in life. The choice of employees has its challenges, but is consistent with Jesus' inclusive view of the kingdom. COOK could make more money than it does, but deliberately devotes time and resources to community projects, such as the provision of 250 meals a day in a church in Chatham, serving disadvantaged people in North Kent.

Witnessing by word

Once they grow beyond a limited size, most companies started by Christians employ people of other faiths or none as well. In order to maintain a consistent ethos, non-Christians need to 'buy into' the Christian values. Several of our entrepreneurs saw positive benefits resulting from it. One said:

> From the start, wherever a role doesn't require a Christian understanding or faith, I've been very keen to have anyone who has the skills inhabit that role. The business has Christians and non-Christians working together and learning to share values. Through the business there is an opportunity to talk about faith. I think in that way it's furthering God's kingdom. People without Christian faith are experiencing Jesus and seeing faith being acted out by colleagues who are Christians. I am keen to encourage that.

This brings us to the third group of entrepreneurs, who saw advancing the kingdom primarily in terms of speaking about their faith to people in the workplace. Few if any saw themselves as direct evangelists; all were aware of the need to be sensitive about time and place. They know too that their words must have credibility. Those words must be supported by the type of people they are and the things they do. But the entrepreneurs in this third group were definitely on the lookout for opportunities to talk about Jesus.

One example is Barry, managing director of a car dealership group. His dealer profile on AM Online (the automotive management website) mentions that he runs the business according to the Christian values of honesty and integrity inherited from his father. Barry says that 'if you are authentically you and a follower of Jesus, in the workplace and not just at home or in church, then you will get into good conversations'. He cited a recent conversation with a colleague who had shared with him a dream that had bothered him. Barry found that a suitable opportunity to invite him to church. If employees are having marriage difficulties, 'we give them six free counselling sessions that we pay for with a Christian counsellor. This is because we honour and believe in marriage. Seeing a Christian counsellor might not mean them becoming Christians, but it might make them more whole, more who they are created to be.'

The group holds a company carol service. Barry finds it immensely satisfying to sit in the service and hear the gospel being preached to large gatherings of employees and their families. 'They are in church out of their own choice! We don't make anyone go; we just say we're putting it on.'

There appears to be something about Christian car dealers and company carol services, because Mark Mitchell also rates this experience highly. Mark says, 'Standing in Chester Cathedral in front of 1,200 people welcoming them at

Christmas: to see all those faces who've supported us for so many years in the commercial setting, then come and celebrate Christmas with us – that's very special. Every time I do that, I'm grateful.'

The fact that Mark's Christian faith is well known means that people often seek him out and ask questions. He described a customer who asked for some advice about a car, but first wanted to talk about faith. He said to Mark: 'I've always been uncertain about faith, but then I look at you and see a guy who works well with a good grasp of business, but has also made sense of faith. I want some of that.' This gave Mark an apt opportunity for witness. His attitude is encapsulated by 1 Peter 3:15: 'Always be ready to make your defence to anyone who demands from you an accounting for the hope that is in you; yet do it with gentleness and reverence.' It is more effective when Christians are asked about their faith than when they feel they have to tell people about their faith.

Direct witness may be easier in some business sectors than others. Adrian is director of a company which supplies fire detection and audio-visual signalling systems to businesses across the world. Its markets include marine engineering, power stations, and oil and gas production plants. Adrian thinks that the UK has become a very hard country in which to be a Christian. He says: 'There is a lot of pressure to keep what you believe to yourself.'

Adrian travels widely in the Far East, and there he has encountered a very different attitude. He says: 'There's a big cultural difference with the Chinese. In England people are shy of talking about their faith; it's not something you talk about in everyday conversation. The Chinese are very open. You can talk about spiritual beliefs or things quite easily.' Adrian recalled a dinner with a Malaysian from a traditional Buddhist Chinese background, who was interested to discover that Adrian was a Christian and keen to learn more. Richard and Kina have both had similar experiences on our separate trips to the Far East. We need to be open to opportunities for witness as and when they arise, which will often include unexpected places.

Our own cultural background may also affect how ready *we* are to share our faith. Caroline Marsh comes from Zambia, worked as an air stewardess and then settled in the UK after getting married. She has worked successfully in property management since 2006. A confident, extrovert woman, her answer to the question about advancing the kingdom was as follows:

> In the property business my business is about people and God's business is about people. We provide high-quality, low-cost accommodation for professionals. I'm giving a service and in my service I make sure I am portraying Christ. We are very friendly and open; my tenants know me and I know them. We sit together from time to time; most invite me to have meals with them. I share God with them and invite them to my local church. Every tenant knows that I am a Christian. Nobody will go a day without my telling them about the kingdom. I need to share the message of the kingdom that God loves you!

Charitable giving

The fourth group of entrepreneurs saw their contribution to the building of God's kingdom mainly in terms of giving to charitable and Christian causes. This was probably the smallest of the four groups, but still significant, and many of the entrepreneurs who did not answer this question in financial terms are also substantial givers. Running a successful business often leads to the accumulation of personal wealth. This gives entrepreneurs the opportunity to be generous. As one said: 'making money and distributing to Christian causes is one way that you're extending God's kingdom.' It recalls the heritage of Christian entrepreneurs who were notable philanthropists.

Giving of this kind often goes well beyond the payment of a tithe – the regular donation of a tenth of one's disposable income. Such a practice provides a good rule of thumb in the early stages of our careers, but many entrepreneurs reach a position where they are able and happy to give away far more than that.

David Capps, who runs a family financial services firm, answered the kingdom question along these lines.

> We have no outside shareholders. We the family own
> it. Everyone who works for us knows that. We're very
> generous to them, we give them bonuses and we give them
> incentives, but we don't give them shares. That maintains
> our independence. So we ultimately have what's left in the
> way of profit. We try to support the kingdom financially,
> and we are particularly strong on that.

Over the years he and his family have supported about twenty-five different charities, most of them involved in Christian outreach by providing practical help in their communities.

LingLing Parnin runs no fewer than five restaurant outlets in Cambridge, all within the busy area near the railway station. She works alongside her husband Franck, who gives his name to one of the restaurants, Le Gros Franck. She is Taiwanese and he is French, a powerful culinary combination! LingLing loves her work – she is always delighted to see customers enjoying their food – but she is especially enthusiastic about the charity that she wholeheartedly supports, The Saints Project Trust.

The trust supports churches, orphanages, schools and relief work in Africa and India; it has a strong emphasis on prayer and spiritual support. LingLing puts a lot of energy into raising money for the trust and visiting its various projects. She has even had a school in south-west Kenya delightfully named after her: the LingLing Beautiful International Guild Academy. Support for the trust is the main way she sees herself advancing the kingdom.

A holistic approach

We believe that the kingdom of God is being advanced in each of these four ways: making the world a better place, embodying Christian values, witnessing by word, and charitable giving. All can be significant ways of bringing God's world more directly under his rule, of being a power for good and reversing the advance of evil. Many admirable things are being done under each of these headings. What we would like to see is entrepreneurs having a broad view of God's kingdom rather than a narrow one. We urge them to embrace all these different categories in a holistic understanding rather than limit themselves to only one.

To be fair, some entrepreneurs we interviewed did straddle the different categories. Phil Schluter, who trades in coffee made in Africa, said this:

> I think God's kingdom is advanced by words, by telling people the gospel when we have the chance. But it also happens through actions, when we look after the poor, widows and orphans, doing the things that Jesus did as part of the kingdom. I am inspired by the vision of heaven in Revelation where there will be no more hunger, thirst, crying or pain. In much of Africa where I visit there is extreme

hunger, pain, crying and suffering. Ultimately we believe the new heaven and new earth are coming but that doesn't stop us doing something now, trying to bring alleviation to the world while we live in it.

A final kingdom-oriented example of social enterprise is MicroEnsure, run by Richard Leftley. Richard gave up a comfortable life in the City when he was challenged by a visit to Zambia and met a woman who was thrown into extreme poverty when her husband died suddenly. He realized that the vast majority of people in the Global South have no insurance system to fall back on. He felt called by God to go about providing one. The result is an insurance system which is remarkably simple, universal and effective. Unlike most insurance systems it is not riddled with exceptions, exclusions and fine print. MicroEnsure's website proclaims Richard's philosophy:

> We know that our customers don't wake up in the morning wanting to purchase insurance, but they do wake up worrying about the risks they face each day. That's why I started MicroEnsure, to help those people around the world who need it most should bad things happen to them.

Richard's answer to the question about God's kingdom was to tell another powerful story about a heart-rending encounter, this one in Bangladesh: a woman who could not get treatment for her sick child because the only provision was a private clinic. She left her child at the clinic, went home, sold everything she had and when she returned the child had died. Richard sat in a shack with this woman and was determined to do something to right the injustice.

For me bringing in God's kingdom is about taking action. I can't change the world and I can't make every woman on every street corner happier, but I can do something and I am doing something about 43 million people. A million people a month are signing up.

MicroEnsure consistently exceeds expectations. It works in countries with Muslims, Hindus, animists, anyone. Richard says:

When these people know we're Christians, come to us and say, 'Why are you here? Why are you helping me? Why are you doing this stuff?' we turn round and say, 'Because our God calls us to love you, to serve you.' That's immensely powerful in terms of evangelism, in terms of showing people the logic of Jesus' love shining in their communities.

Does your business provide a powerful witness by accompanying words with actions?

Seek ye first . . .

Among the Bible passages that entrepreneurs found most motivating, Matthew 6:33 ranked near the top. It is best known in the old Authorized Version. 'Seek ye first the kingdom of God, and his righteousness, and all these things shall be added unto you.' 'These things' refer to the essentials of food and clothing. The kingdom of God exerts a strong pull upon us. We may not fully understand everything that is entailed in the kingdom, but we know it commands our allegiance. We must not ignore the phrase that follows – 'and his righteousness' – and we shall attend to that in chapter 11. With that proviso in mind, Jesus assures us that if we make his kingdom our priority, he will attend to our basic needs.

7. YOU NEED A GUT DESIRE

Jeremy Higham and his wife run a film-making company. They specialize in making films for all kinds of companies and organizations. Their website explains: 'We create short films that captivate and inspire, expressing and celebrating what's distinct about your business, helping you to be understood.'

What is striking about Jeremy is that he has a vision not only for his own business but also for other people's business. He partners his clients in helping them to articulate their vision, embodying it in memorable images and scenarios designed to help the viewer connect quickly with the essence of the organization.

Jeremy believes that people were 'created by God to honour him and benefit the earth. We are children of the creative generative God, enabled to be creative and generative ourselves. In the same way that he made kingfishers and mountains, we have the built-in imagination to imagine the things that do not currently exist and bring them into being – in cooperation with others.' Objects that benefit others include most things made by business, if done well: 'a wonderful fruit drink that will refresh people, or a great toaster that will last'. They also include 'making films like we do, films that remind companies of who they are, and encourage them to express themselves confidently and clearly, without trying too hard to self-promote'.

Jeremy's vision is one of *re-enchantment*. 'A while ago I felt God say that he would use us to re-enchant the business world. That word means "get it singing again".' Jeremy longs to hear the outbreak of more singing in factories and corporate boardrooms, as people 'celebrate the joy of work because they understand the value of what they're doing'. His is a powerful vision which has the potential to inspire the business world as a whole. Some companies do not fully appreciate the good work they are already doing. Jeremy wants them to wake up to what that is and proclaim it.

Fearfully and wonderfully made; beautiful inside and out

We have already introduced two female entrepreneurs who work in fashion design. The vision for Rebeca Li's work revolves round a verse in Psalm 139. When Rebeca is wearing a dress she feels good in, she echoes the psalmist: 'I praise you, for I am fearfully and wonderfully made' (Psalm 139:14). She also has this conviction about her clients: she wants them to feel that same God-given sense of wonder when wearing the clothes she designs for them.

Rebeca told the story of designing a dress for a friend, Anna. She felt that Anna's wardrobe did not display the personality of the real person. It was all rather functional and restrained. A photo on her bedside table of Anna as a young girl offered a clue to a different side of her. Rebeca realized that it would be counterproductive to clothe Anna in a bold colour like purple, but she wanted to extend her range. 'I put her in a winter colour with sensitivity because she can't be pushed too far. She put the dress on and she looked beautiful: everybody commented.' Rebeca had designed a dress for Anna that made her shine as God intended.

Rebeca recognizes that fashion has its superficial side. This is evident in the search for good-looking men and women to be models. Rebeca comments:

> God made me to be sincere. God made me to be a woman with heart, love, seeing other people in God's image. But in the creative arts and fashion there is so much temptation to be superficial. I declare that I have been made in God's image. I have been made to respect and honour other human beings as made in God's image, rather than to view them superficially, to judge a model just as someone who's pretty.

This is the vision that inspires her work.

We have shown how the vision of Natasha Rufus Isaacs and Beulah is to create a space where women feel beautiful inside and out, and then experience the love of God. By offering an ethical fashion store, Natasha seeks to impact the lives both of rich Western women and of women much poorer and less privileged than themselves.

Beulah's vision extends to some very practical outcomes. Natasha woke up one morning with a picture of lots of blue hearts. She immediately thought of the United Nations anti-trafficking campaign, which uses a blue heart as a logo. She decided to give 10% of profits from Beulah's blue scarves (their most popular scarf) to the United Nations campaign.

Rebeca and Natasha are *passionate* people. Rebeca said:

> Yesterday I was introduced at a fashion show by a close friend,
> and she described me as a person with passion. When people
> come across me they say they can't help but be hooked in!
> People want to come with me and help me, work for me.
> I think that's a God-given property.

For Natasha, what gets her up in the morning is her passion
for the business. 'I love what I do. Although it is very hard
work and very stressful, I have a real passion for making a
difference, for reaching women in our world.' Both trans-
parently mean what they say.

Bringing joy

Designing beautiful clothes for people can bring great satisfaction, for the designer and the recipient. Many other material
objects can do that as well.

Richard's son Peter is a solo entrepreneur, a carpenter who
has set up his own business. He explains on his website:

> My company is called Carpintree. I love being a maker.
> With you we can create custom cabinetry, bespoke joinery and
> handmade furniture for your home, boat or public place. If you
> want something unique, a one-off, or to copy existing pieces,
> I am your man. I have always been a woodworker. With over
> 20,000 hours on the tools, in the last ten years I have been
> busy. From work in Norwich Cathedral and King's College
> Cambridge, to local churches and family homes, classic yachts
> and not forgetting some giant pencils. I have worked alongside
> some of the strongest shipwrights in the West Country and
> taught some of the most dedicated ladyboys in Cambodia.

The photographs on Peter's website confirm the quality of his work. They include a beautifully carved table, distinctively built with three legs which have the names of the Trinity – Father, Son, Spirit – inscribed upon them. That is now used to celebrate Communion in St Barnabas Church, Cambridge.

When asked, 'What was your most satisfying moment as an entrepreneur?' Peter replied:

> Among particular jobs, some front doors I did recently.
> These went beyond the customer's expectations and gave
> him lots of joy. In that job I pulled different facets together
> in a satisfying way. For me joy is found in making things
> and passing them on rather than having them and constantly
> seeing them.

It is joy – the smile of delight on a customer's face – which motivates and sustains Peter in his work.

Sadly, many take the beauty of material objects too much for granted. Christians can be particularly prone to this, because we are taught to be so suspicious of materialism. Look round the room in which you are probably reading this book. Take in the chairs, tables, lamps, TV, books, DVDs, windows, doors, shelves, cupboards and cushions. Behind the appearance of everyday objects lie the efforts of ingenious entrepreneurs.

All-metal connection hoses

It is easy to understand the excitement and vision that surround the creation of silk dresses and three-legged Communion tables. However, much business activity concerns the creation, delivery and fitting of more prosaic objects. Take the flexible metal hoses which connect your domestic gas meter. Could anyone get excited about those? The answer is yes, and we are delighted to know the man whose firm makes most of them: David Runton.

David has lived all his life in the West Riding of Yorkshire. He started his career as an accountant, visited companies he audited, and became interested in how they worked. He asked questions on the shop floor, observed what was successful and compared different styles of management.

David was particularly interested in FTL, an engineering company which was struggling with no orders. He had a vision of how he could make it work, and in 1968 was asked by the client to join the company. David believed he could make all-metal connection hoses that would service steel, chemical and gas industries and general engineering. Early on he identified what would give FTL competitive advantage. His aim was to be one of the top three companies in the UK in that particular sector.

David developed three discrete but interconnected business aims. They were to develop the business (measured in financial terms), to develop people (understood as developing their talents), and to achieve high standards of quality, reliability and delivery (measured by customer satisfaction). FTL made rapid progress and was successfully marketing gas meter connectors by the end of 1972.

In 1973 David started a second company, FTL Seals Technology, which was an offshoot of the hose business. It provided consultancy and supply of high-pressure seals in hydraulic applications. This business took longer to get going. In David's words, comparing their experience to that of Joseph in Egypt, 'we had a full seven lean years of losses (1973–80) before the business started making money'. But things worked out well overall. David said:

In the 1970s, when the seals technology company was struggling to get off the ground, we were upheld by the hose business doing well. In the 1980s it was the other way round. As a result of the economic downturn in the UK and a decline in the fortunes of some of our main customers, the hose company made three years of losses, but the seals technology company took off.

David believes that, under his leadership, FTL stood out for its proactive rather than reactive approach to its industrial customers. The company sought to discuss a customer's business development issues, even asking questions about what the customer's customers were doing. With this additional knowledge, FTL was able to anticipate the customer's needs and provide a better service. It went out of its way to please the customer, to exceed the customer's expectations.

David too talks about his business in a passionate way, though he prefers the language of desire. 'I think there's something quite physical about being an entrepreneur. You have to have a desire.' He points to his stomach: 'It is, you know, a gut desire. Because the first thing you come across are obstacles. There are always difficulties or impossibilities and you have to overcome those. It's the strength of your desire that says, "I'm going to overcome them."'

David was a Christian from the time he started as an entrepreneur. He always sought to behave ethically in business and there were areas of behaviour he determinedly avoided. However, he admits he did not consciously integrate his faith into his business practices until he attended a Faith in Business (then called God on Monday) course at Ridley Hall in 1991. 'After that I more consciously offered my work to God. I opened myself up and thanked God for what he had done in the past for me, without my quite realizing it. I committed big or uncomfortable decisions to God in prayer.'

From then on David thought of God as a shareholder in the business. This made him ready to give away more of the wealth he had accrued. Challenged by passages in James (2:15–16) and 1 John (4:21) that call for love to be practical, he set up a charity called the John James Trust. He is delighted that eventually he sold his companies to management he had developed over twenty-five and thirty years, respectively. Both have continued to flourish under managers who learned about entrepreneurship from him.

David's story makes clear that a product that appears mundane and functional can actually engender enormous passion. We experienced something similar with Tony Hodges, who is a communications consultant in the pensions industry. That may not sound very exciting, but Tony speaks with tremendous enthusiasm about it. Of all the people we interviewed, he is perhaps the one who moves fastest in terms of spontaneous action: 'I have a vision and I will move towards it straightaway. I try to move very quickly but also to stop very quickly if God is saying don't go that way.' Tony's vision is one of helping people to be educated so that they can plan effectively for their retirement. He has developed a way of planning which involves a 'highly visual mathematical model'. Anthony Hodges Consulting has become a world leader in the use of this model, so that '12,000 miles away a state government in Queensland, Australia, will appoint us to do a quarter-of-a-million-dollar project'. Tony is convinced that understanding pensions better and making wise decisions on the basis of that knowledge can have a life-transforming effect.

A vision for business

Some of us may be more visionary than others. Some of us work things out in a piecemeal sort of way as we go along.

But it is difficult, if not impossible, to be a successful entrepreneur without having some picture at the outset of what we hope to achieve.

There are certain worthy aims which are common to all types of business. In his excellent book *Why Business Matters to God*, Jeff Van Duzer has set out two important goals which should feature prominently in the vision of any Christian entrepreneur: (1) to provide the community with goods and services that will enable it to flourish, and (2) to provide opportunities for meaningful work that will enable employees to express their God-given creativity. Around those two generic goals, there are many specific visions which will gather. God has instilled individual entrepreneurs with particular enthusiasms, passions and desires. He has given us a vision of a world which is changed for the better through the distinctive good or service we have to offer. If this enthusiasm and the skills or talents to deliver these goods or services are genuinely from God, we should definitely run with this. Our fifty interviewees are people who have done that. Pursuing a distinctive vision as an entrepreneur is an opportunity to play a special part in God's purposes and bring glory to his name.

8. I TAKE CALCULATED RISKS

Most of the entrepreneurs we interviewed considered themselves creative. This is not surprising, given the centrality of creativity to the entrepreneurial process. They saw themselves as people who come up with new ideas and want to explore new ways of doing things.

An entrepreneur who has thought deeply about creativity at a theological level is John Lovatt, who lives near Stoke-on-Trent. He has spent a lifetime running Acme Marls Ltd, a family business in the ceramics industry, specializing in kiln furniture. John has undertaken five distinct ventures in ceramics. At the height of its influence Acme Marls supplied the expanding Chinese market with several turnkey plants (where the contractor has responsibility for the whole delivery of the project), including the ceramic tiles and tableware.

John sees his business expertise and creativity as part of God's creativity.

God is interested in the improvement of my business
expertise, because all creation belongs to him and is created
through him. The exercise of business expertise glorifies God
as its creator. If therefore it is used for evil ends, this is a form
of blasphemy – the misuse of the word of the creator for evil
ends. So God's creativity and my creativity are one.

John says: 'What I find rewarding is creation out of nothing.
For example, there was no factory and now there is.' That is
incredibly satisfying.

John is keenly aware that, in the manufacturing process,
many faulty products are made and have to be rejected.
Corresponding to his all-embracing view of creation is a
holistic view of redemption. The defective products will be
restored and made whole in God's new creation. John bases
this belief on two important New Testament passages:

> For the creation was subjected to futility, not of its own will
> but by the will of the one who subjected it, in hope that the
> creation itself will be set free from its bondage to decay and
> will obtain the freedom of the glory of the children of God.
> (Romans 8:20–21)

> Through him [Christ] God was pleased to reconcile to himself
> all things, whether on earth or in heaven, by making peace
> through the blood of his cross.
> (Colossians 1:20)

God's redemption plan encompasses material things as well
as human beings.

Colossians 1:15–20 is a passage which also inspires Jody
Wainwright. Jody is a Director of Boodles, which has been
making and selling high-quality jewellery since 1798. He

spends most of his time discovering and acquiring diamonds and precious gemstones from all over the world. Jody is excited by the thought that 'all things hold together' in Christ (Colossians 1:17). This gives him courage to act boldly rather than 'just trundle along'.

Jody says that his business is purely about creation – creating jewellery. However, he admits that 'I myself am not very creative'. Instead he employs people who are. 'We have four designers in the house. They're very creative; they're drawing all day long, making beautiful designs, but it's not my strength.' Jody says that 'Rebecca, our head designer, is probably the most important person in our company. She's creating our business brand and image. At the end of the day it's about the quality of the product.'

Jody's contribution is to see what will sell. 'My side of it is to decide "yes, I think that looks like a seller" or "no, that piece of jewellery is not quite right for these reasons".' Having made a decision to back a product, he does so wholeheartedly. He communicates excitement about the beautiful products that Rebecca and others design.

Innovation – from design to market

As we said earlier, creativity by itself does not constitute an entrepreneur. The creative idea needs to be translated into commercial reality. An entrepreneur who makes *his* business out of helping other entrepreneurs do precisely that is Phil Staunton. He is the Managing Director of D2M Innovation, based in Cheltenham. D2M stands for Design to Market. D2M is a specialist innovation company with a passion for helping to develop, prototype, manufacture and protect new concepts. It therefore covers the entire process of bringing a bright idea to fruition. In Phil's words, what D2M offers is 'a one-stop shop for the concept right the way through to patenting, package, branding and products on the shop shelves'. D2M do styling, computer design work, sourcing of a manufacturer, testing and modification of design.

At D2M Innovation, Phil has assembled a formidable team of people with specialist expertise. One exciting project has been to develop a car seat that turns into a buggy. This avoids the troublesome process of transferring a small child from one to the other, often a recipe for tears. Phil worked out a way of fitting the car seat stroller into the limited space of a car and opening it up easily, working with a test house on crash testing. The result is a very stylish product.

Phil sees innovation as absolutely central to his business. 'We are continually on the lookout for new ways to do things. We've always got three or four creative new ideas for improving the service we offer on the go at any one time.' The challenge he faces, ironically, is the need sometimes to rein back this creativity. 'If you are constantly pouring time and resources into improving everything all the time, that sucks the resources out of the company, so we have to manage that and do it in a more controlled fashion.' Nevertheless, D2M has built a brand reputation for being highly innovative.

Phil is upfront about the fact that he is a Christian. His profile on the company website includes the fact that he is an active member of Trinity Church in Cheltenham. He is driven by a desire to 'see people achieve their potential, whether that be as staff who work for me, as clients, so that their new innovative ideas achieve their market potential, or as suppliers, ensuring that they are doing all that they possibly can'. He wants to see all of them flourish, 'even if they don't know God or are unaware that what's within them has come from him'. Do you have as positive a vision as that for your business partners?

Risk-taking

Even when an excellent idea has been thoroughly researched and tested – perhaps by a firm like D2M – there is no guarantee that it will be a commercial success. It is still a risk to launch out as an entrepreneur, especially when a substantial amount of money is invested in the venture. One interviewee, Jyoti Banerjee, said this: 'I can't see how you can be an entrepreneur and not be a risk-taker. Risk-taking is where you have an understanding of how limited your resources are, along with what you are seeking to achieve and what change you want to see happen.'

We asked the question: 'Do you see yourself as a risk-taker? If so, how is this related to being a Christian?' Only one of our fifty said he was not by nature a risk-taker. His self-confessed 'safety first attitude to life' is reflected in the fact that he spent most of his career working for large organizations. It is only in the later stages of his career that he has taken some risks in launching out with a distinctive style of consultancy.

In contrast, several of our sample described themselves as risk-takers without any qualification. This was usually linked to a faith that God would sustain and protect them in whatever they were undertaking. These are quotes from four entrepreneurs:

- 'I didn't see my business as a risk. I was confident because I knew that God loved me.'
- 'I love risk. I believe that the steps of the righteous man are guided by the Lord.'
- 'If you are doing something because God has told you, it's not really a risk. It's more dangerous not to listen to what God says and not take the risk.'

- 'I am a risk-taker. The difference in being a Christian
  may be that you trust in God knowing that he
  will catch and care for us. If he's calling us to
  something and we feel called then we shouldn't
  say no.'

The much more typical response, however, was to affirm
risk, but with a significant degree of qualification. The phrase
'calculated risk' or its equivalent recurred frequently. Consider
the following:

- 'If you don't take risks you're not an entrepreneur.
  But you try to limit risks or manage them.'
- 'I am a cautious and calculated risk-taker. I take risks
  after a lot of analysis.'
- 'I am a risk-taker but I also have a brain. So I take risks
  but they are calculated.'
- 'I try to take smart risks, not stupid risks. Taking on
  a workshop which I repaired and fitted was a risk, but
  it turned out to be a good decision.'
- 'I take measured risks. A few years ago we made a
  decision to invest just over £1 million in a new product
  range. It was right.'
- 'I take calculated risks. I always like to step back and
  reflect and mull for a while. Sometimes I do this during
  church services.'
- 'Faith is taking a risk. Putting trust in God allows us
  to take prudent risks.'
- 'I'm a calculating risk-taker. The size of risk varies at
  different stages of the business. As a Christian there is
  a greater ultimate confidence in God, but sometimes
  as Christians we do things that are less risky because
  God makes us wise.'

The similarity of response is striking, far greater than with most of the questions we asked. Christian entrepreneurs affirm risk but in a discriminating sort of way. Several spoke of the need for *discernment*. We need to discern between different types of project. Some definitely entail risk; they stretch our resources and test our faith, but the Holy Spirit is prompting us to go ahead, confident that God will bless our endeavour. Others are plain foolish. They fly in the face of economic reality and established market trends. We should avoid them.

A critical friend

Some of the most interesting reflection on discernment and risk came from Nigel Walter. He is an architect, the founding Director of Archangel, a practice which specializes in church work, particularly in helping church communities make a better fit between their buildings and their ministries. Within a few years, three Anglican churches near the centre of Cambridge – St Philip's, St Barnabas' and St Paul's – have had their interiors transformed under his expert care and direction. In all three cases, this has not only improved the quality of the worship experience but opened the buildings up for use by local community groups. Nigel said:

> Part of my skill set is being able to listen – I used to be
> a counsellor alongside doing architecture. The process of
> creating buildings or changing buildings should involve a lot
> of listening, because it is about getting to what clients want,
> which they may not be able to express. It is trying to reach the
> existential landscape behind the particular request. A church
> may say we want to get rid of the pews. Usually the important
> issue is not the pews themselves, but what lies behind the
> surface – perhaps a yearning for more flexibility of worship,

or a change of mission strategy, or simply liturgical taste. Understanding that hinterland is essential.

In affirming that he was a risk-taker, Nigel continued:

> Part of my frustration is because I see quite a lot of churches that are terrified of risk. There is a certain mindset that we can't possibly take a risk because something might go wrong. For me, risk is almost synonymous with life. If you can't take risks you are not alive any more. The issue is not whether to take risks, but which risks you choose to take, and taking those risks well.

Nigel compared his role as an architect with being invited to join a group on a journey.

> You are invited on the journey because you have knowledge or experience that they know they lack, but need. I see our role as being a critical friend for the duration of that journey. That sometimes means challenging people. If you're not able to challenge your clients you are not doing your job, and that involves taking risk for yourself – ultimately, you may lose the job. But in the end, it is the client's project, not yours, and it is just as important to know when to stop challenging: 'a time to speak, and a time to remain silent'.

Nigel is clearly adept in the art of challenging clients, because he has successfully persuaded many to change their buildings in radical ways.

Strong and courageous

Taking risks requires the quality of *courage*. Among the characteristics that our Christian entrepreneurs identified, courage featured quite prominently. However, it is not only relevant with regard to the making of big decisions. Courage is required on a regular, even daily basis in the practice of business. We often need to be brave in our handling of relationships. Business can be a tough place, where sharp things are said and the strong exploit the weak. There are individuals who need challenging and confronting; they may be employees, they may be customers, they may be business partners.

Gareth Mulholland is the founder-director of Eden Ecommerce Ltd, an internet business which 'showcases and sells works of literature, music and art that will equip, inspire and encourage people in Christian life, mission and worship'. It has fifty staff and half a million customers in the UK, testimony to its substantial growth in the past ten years. But like other online businesses, notably Amazon, it is unpopular with some who regard e-commerce as threatening the livelihoods of those who work on the high street.

Gareth understands courage as 'the knowledge that God is behind me, God is there. So I have courage to do the right thing, fearing less the human side of things and what might happen. I would rather be doing what I think God wants me to do, because that's why I'm on this planet, the reason I am alive, than not to do it.'

An important aspect of courage is facing up to the worst that might happen and being prepared to live with it. Jeweller Jody also alluded to this when he cited a favourite verse, Psalm 112:7, which says that the righteous 'are not afraid of evil tidings; their hearts are firm, secure in the LORD'. Jody feels this is crucial because there are always disappointments in business. 'There are ten reasons why something won't work, when there are only two reasons why it will. But if one of the two reasons is that God has told you to do something, what is there to fear? Are you seeing God in all his greatness?'

Courage was singled out as important by the younger entrepreneurs we interviewed. Perhaps this was because they had to fight for recognition from older people in business. Fashion designer Natasha showed courage in starting Beulah in her mid-twenties with no previous business experience. Carpenter Peter received little encouragement from his supervisor and experienced fear as an apprentice, but has realized that the quality of his work carries respect and he has no need to fear anyone.

However, one of the most courageous acts we heard about was a management buyout. It was led by Keith Noronha, now Managing Director of Reynolds Technology. This Birmingham-based company manufactures and supplies steel tubing for bicycle frames and other bicycle components. Twenty-seven winners of the Tour de France have used bicycles with Reynolds tubing.

The company dates back to its establishment by John Reynolds in 1898. By the 1990s it had been taken over by some Americans, but hit hard times and in 2000 was threatened with closure. The owners were running out of money and eager to sell. Keith had worked for Reynolds from 1996 onwards as a senior manager; he is an ardent cycling enthusiast and was keen to save the company. Along with four others, he organized a management buyout. Keith took the decision to do this very quickly, 'within a week or two'; otherwise the opportunity would have been lost irretrievably.

In Keith's own words:

I was interested in the business and our family basically raised the funds to buy it. We recognized the danger that it could be a sinkhole: you put the money in and it goes down the plug-hole. Privately financing an enterprise like this can be very stressful. So it was for myself, my

family and my wife; at the time it affected many things
we did.

He feels that his faith helped to reduce the stress. Going to
church helped him to unwind, reconnect and set the stress of
the business world in a wider perspective. Although the period
of arranging the buyout and re-establishing the company was
extremely tough, Keith feels going through that made him
mentally stronger. He grew in courage. After several difficult
trading years in the 2000s, Reynolds Technology is doing well
with a much-increased turnover.

'Be strong and courageous; do not be frightened or dis-
mayed, for the LORD your God is with you wherever you go'
(Joshua 1:9). God's words to Joshua on the verge of entering
the Promised Land are highly relevant to many an entrepreneurial venture. Do you need to make a conscious effort to
take courage?

9. STAKEHOLDERS, SERVANTS AND SHEPHERDS

Alongside our research into Christian entrepreneurs, Faith in Business has co-partnered with the Jubilee Centre and the London Institute for Contemporary Christianity on a closely related research project. Whereas the primary focus of the research we conducted is entrepreneurs' motivation, the centre of interest in this joint project is the preservation of a company's Christian ethos. How does a company started by Christians ensure that ethos really sticks?

In this project, executives from eight companies were interviewed to explore how – over a sustained period of time – Christian faith has influenced those companies' goals, values and working practices. The report was published in April 2016 as *The Resilient Business: Embedding Christian Values in Your Company's DNA.*

The key point to emerge from the research is that a Christian ethos will only be maintained by close attention to relationships. The report explains the way these eight companies have nurtured relationships with business owners, staff, customers, suppliers, neighbours and the environment. Four of the eight companies researched for this project coincide with four entrepreneurs we interviewed.

We certainly agree that relationships with stakeholders (all the different groups who have a 'stake' in what a company does) are of prime importance in business. Indeed, Faith in Business held a weekend conference focusing on this very theme in April 2016. The Christian entrepreneurs we interviewed are overwhelmingly 'people' people. Concern for the quality of relationships lies at the very heart of what they are about.

There is general agreement among businesspeople, Christians included, that all the different stakeholders matter. But do some relationships matter more than others? This was not a question we asked explicitly, yet some sense of order emerged from the way they discussed their business. Where the business was small – in particular, where entrepreneurs were operating mainly on their own – relationships with customers loomed large. Where the business was larger, and responsible for employing a sizeable number of staff, then relationships with employees dominated. Most of our fifty entrepreneurs were in the second category.

Boots and Bibles

Mark Mitchell boldly stated: 'Our employees are more important than our customers. I am afraid the customer doesn't come first!' He commented on how important it is to bring people on in their careers and encourage them every day. Mark personally recruited all his team of 104; he knows their names, as well as their partners' and children's names, and invites all of them on an annual boat trip – even their dogs. He says:

I operate a really strong pastoral safety net. I'm conscious that I am the closest many of our staff will get to meeting a church leader or pastor, so I have to be there for them. Just because you work for our business doesn't mean you're immune from the challenges life throws at you. So at the moment, we have three marriages in free-fall, we have some terminal illness and one of my team has run up credit card debts of £27,000. In some respects I'm a pastor.

Mark draws inspiration from the Cadbury brothers, who gave employees a Bible on their wedding day. Fewer people get married these days, so Mark and Anita have hit on a different way to get the Bible into people's homes. They ask to visit all the newborn babies in the business. They take with them a children's Bible and a pair of boots as gifts. Mark explains:

We take a beautiful pair of blue or pink Wellington boots. They're 'designer', which I make no apology for, they're expensive, they're French and they're beautiful. Newborn babies obviously can't walk for twelve months, but they sit there symbolically by the fireplace until the child can walk. A Bible by itself would be heavy handed, the Wellington boots are a lovely icebreaker. The two together are perfect.

Putting employees first does not mean the customer comes a poor second best. On the contrary, the Mitchell Group takes pleasure in its high levels of customer satisfaction. So the customer waiting areas are immaculately clean and spacious, replete with television screens, internet cafés and complimentary refreshment areas. Well-trained hosts match customers with the salesperson they think will connect with them best. There are several women on the sales team so that female customers who come in on their own do not feel intimidated. The Mitchell Group offers exceptional service.

There is a paradox here, because cars now are so reliable that a dealer can often go a long time before seeing customers again, which creates the challenge of how to keep in touch with them. Mark hit on the idea of offering people who bought a car from the Mitchell Group a free car wash every Saturday for the rest of their lives. 'So last Saturday we washed 187 cars in four hours, between 8.30 and 12.30.' Mark definitely has the statistics all worked out.

> There are two or two and a half people in each car, so we had 450 guests in the business last week. They're used to coming in and they're familiar. We make a note of every car registration number and the mileage when they come in. With people who are a little bit past their service date, we'll ring them on the Monday morning and say, 'It was great to see you on Saturday. We hope we washed your car well. As a duty of care, we just want to tell you that your car needs a service.'

There speaks a true salesman. Keeping the relationship alive and warm means that customers are more likely to return when the time comes to change their car.

Lunch or banquet?

Lawsons is a family business, founded in 1921. It is the largest independent timber, building materials and fencing merchant in the south-east of England. In 1990 Simon joined the business, succeeding his father John who is son and grandson of the founders. Simon Lawson is now Chairman. He has modernized the branches and developed a speciality in the loft conversion market.

Lawsons' strapline is 'Family values – professional service', and its mission statement is 'To make work as interesting and satisfying as possible'. This indicates a strong focus on employee welfare. The benefits the company offers exceed most in that industry sector:

- an income protection scheme for five years in the case of illness
- a death-in-service benefit
- a contributory pension scheme and profit-share scheme
- financial, legal and relationship counselling and support
- childcare vouchers
- a scheme to enable the purchase of a bike to travel to work
- store vouchers and gifts on significant life occasions, such as a wedding or the birth of a child.

Simon, whose Christian background is Quaker, is keenly aware that for many people, genuine community is in short supply. In his workplace he seeks to provide the sense of stability, security and belonging that he sees as largely lacking in society.

When asked what characterizes him as a Christian entrepreneur, Simon says it is 'an acknowledgment that all my success is due to God'. This echoes Deuteronomy 8:18: 'Remember the LORD your God, for it is he who gives you power to get wealth.' Simon is a humble man, believing that meekness (Matthew 5:5) is an important quality to avoid the trap of hubris that often comes with business success. He expresses his role in terms of servant leadership, a model of leadership strongly associated with the US author Robert

Greenleaf, but which is vividly portrayed in the earthly ministry of Jesus, particularly the washing of his disciples' feet. Consider John 13:14–17:

> So if I, your Lord and Teacher, have washed your feet, you also ought to wash one another's feet. For I have set you an example, that you also should do as I have done to you.

Simon connects very much with this story and seeks to follow it through. His servant heart is particularly evident in the most unusual and distinctive way he exercises leadership: the 'values lunches' that he hosts on a regular basis – four times a year over the past five years. These are given not on company premises, but at Simon's own home; the catering is not outsourced, but Simon himself cooks and serves the food. He invites different employees each time and asks them what they would like to eat. Not only that, he also asks them what they would like to talk about. 'I have no agenda, it's their agenda.' They talk about anything they want: football, life experiences, how the business and its values can improve the common good, what makes the employees feel valued, and what it feels like working on the front line.

It is difficult to be vulnerable in the workplace, especially when you are the boss, but Simon makes a conscious effort to be vulnerable. During the values lunches he talks about some of the life challenges he has faced himself, including his experience of divorce and what it is like to be a single father. The problems he discusses are things that many of his employees wrestle with as well. Putting himself on the spot enables Simon and his employees to build relationships of mutual trust. It is clear that these values lunches are enormously appreciated.

When lunches are permeated by this degree of openness, when people are truly authentic, they are very special events indeed. Less like a lunch and more like a banquet!

Care and confrontation

Servant is one key biblical model of leadership. Shepherd is another. It is actually the most frequent image used of leaders, prominent in both Old and New Testaments. It seems rather an unfashionable image now, since it carries agricultural and paternalistic overtones, but one of our entrepreneurs, David Runton, has consciously practised a shepherd style of leadership. Again, this is based on the teaching of Jesus, in John 10:2–4:

> The one who enters by the gate is the shepherd of the sheep. The gatekeeper opens the gate for him, and the sheep hear his voice. He calls his own sheep by name and leads them out. When he has brought out all his own, he goes ahead of them, and the sheep follow him because they know his voice.

Several years ago Richard accompanied David as he made a morning tour of his company, FTL. Here were employees who knew their leader's voice. David knew the names of everyone, politely and genuinely inquiring not just about their work but about their health and that of their families. For him the essence of the shepherd model is that the leader shows the way while demonstrating a close and genuine interest in his 'flock'.

Now semi-retired, David continues to be challenged by the risen Christ's words to Peter: 'Feed my lambs' (John 21:15). The form this now takes is ringing people up for a chat:

I have a thing that I call 'Cheer up Monday' – as prayer directs me I try to ring friends up on a Monday when I know they're going through some difficulty. My purpose is to hear their voice and for them to hear mine, so they don't feel like a lost or forgotten sheep.

A shepherd style of leader might sound like someone who is a soft touch. That is far from being the case. In biblical times, shepherding was a demanding and hazardous occupation. Danger lurked in the valleys in the form of robbers and wild beasts. We know from Psalm 23 that the shepherd had a rod, probably a cudgel in his belt, for beating off attackers. In a modern organizational context, leaders may need to be similarly vigilant and courageous to protect a company and its staff from external attack.

David Runton told a fascinating story about a difficult customer that FTL supplied in the 1980s. This corporate client was, for a time, impossible to please. FTL's deliveries were persistently rejected, the allegation being that they were 'not to specification'. David knew that these charges were unjust. He became so disenchanted that he was ready to terminate the relationship. So he drove to the company's head office and told the customer that he had had enough. A little while later the relationship did resume when the customer came back, 'dragging its tail', and offered both to take a less critical attitude and even to pay FTL more for the products. David agreed. An improvement in the relationship followed which lasted several years.

Some time later, however, a change in customer ownership was followed by another barrage of complaints. It looked as if history was repeating itself, but David recognized that this time the situation was different. FTL had gone though a difficult patch, and quality of service was no longer as good as it had been. Again he drove to the company's head office – this time to apologize, not to confront. A constructive discussion followed about how FTL could serve the customer better.

The story illustrates how every situation needs to be judged on its merits. As entrepreneurs we should not be locked into one way of reacting. David surely deserves credit for his courage on both occasions, first for confronting the customer when FTL was *not* at fault, and second for saying sorry when it *was* at fault. Both initiatives he took were unusual, but led to some very positive outcomes. Many years on, this customer still does regular business with FTL.

Loyalty

Most of the entrepreneurs we interviewed had been through hard times. Sales plummet, cash runs out and, with the best will in the world, it appears impossible to keep all the company's stakeholders happy. It becomes very tempting – in the words of one entrepreneur – to say, 'God, I've had enough. I just want to switch off, accept that the company closes down, go find another job and work for a large corporate.'

Keith Noronha faced that situation in the years after taking over at Reynolds Technology. 'Sales between 2003 and 2005 fell a lot. We were running out of cash. I borrowed pretty much all the money I could just to keep the business going, and had lots of sleepless nights. We came very close to closing the company down.' What kept Keith going? Essentially, a deep sense of loyalty to the men who worked for him.

In a small firm you get to know the people, you know their families and you know their hobbies. These guys had worked

for us for a long time. If we closed the business, their age
meant it would have been very difficult for them to get
another job. It was different for me. I could still start again,
because of my qualifications. The responsibility I felt to
semi-skilled guys in Birmingham weighed very heavily upon
me, and in the end led me to keep going. But my faith also
had an impact.

Another dimension of those difficult days was the cash-flow
challenge of paying suppliers. There were times when Keith
ordered something from a supplier and did not know how he
was going to foot the bill. But somehow, he says, 'we paid
every single supplier that we owed money to'. However, they
were helped by a supplier's understanding attitude in some
cases. Keith had a frank conversation about his company's
difficulties with a company in Germany who sell a particular
type of steel. Being honest about Reynolds' problems was a
humbling experience for Keith, but it actually proved bene-
ficial. He recalls that 'they worked through the problem with
us', negotiating delayed payment, which bought Reynolds
some valuable time. Often it is the loyalty of a business partner
that helps an entrepreneur to survive.

Treating suppliers fairly

The relationship a company has with its suppliers warrants
further attention. This is probably the stakeholder relationship
that the public thinks about least, but for those in business it is
of crucial importance. 'It is problems in the supply chain that
keep you awake worrying at night,' said one entrepreneur.

In the big corporate world, relationships between companies and their suppliers easily assume an adversarial nature.
Although in theory the relationship is one of partnership, in

practice one party often seeks to exploit the other. So corporate customers frequently:

- rely on a large number of suppliers, playing them off against one another to gain price concessions;
- use only short-term contracts, with good performance being no guarantee of their renewal;
- focus on price to the neglect of other factors;
- pay suppliers late, causing cash-flow problems;
- are quick to blame and penalize suppliers when difficulties arise.

One of the UK's leading supermarkets, for example, has achieved notoriety for its perceived policy of 'screwing the supplier'.

John Carlisle is a consultant who has made it his life's goal to improve customer–supplier relationships. Back in the early 1980s, he hit on the truth that collaborative organizations make more money. He worked out 'a strategy for bringing contractors, suppliers and clients together in projects based on amicable relationships'. His company became the largest in Europe at providing major projects with collaborative strategies. In 2002, their client the Hong Kong Metro completed its rail extension project four months early and £1.5 billion under budget. John is the co-author of *Beyond Negotiation: Redeeming Customer–Supplier Relationships*.

In general the entrepreneurs whom we interviewed saw suppliers much more as partners than as adversaries, though the temptation to assume the tough adversarial model increases the larger a company grows. An attitude of care for the supplier was most evident in those doing business with companies in the Global South. This is not surprising, because the goal of improving the nature of the supply chain is part of their *raison d'être*. Phil Schluter's coffee trading company is not technically a fair-trade company, but it shares much of the same outlook with companies that are designated as 'fair trade'. Phil sees one of his firm's priorities as being

> to divide the significant profit margin between the commodity price of coffee in Africa and the selling price in the West to leave a greater share of the value in the hands of the producers: a voluntary relinquishing of market power.
> The vision of the firm is 'to transform lives in Africa through mutually profitable commerce'.

Ramona Hirschi is founder and Managing Director of Little Trove, a fair-trade company based in Newcastle-under-Lyme. She is Malaysian and her husband Raphael, who helps with the business, is Swiss. Little Trove specializes in home décor gifts such as cushions, vases, candles and enamelware. As Ramona says on her website: 'Sometimes, it seems that modern business has forgotten what it means to be fair. We believe that others don't exist to make us rich – we exist to enrich others. We believe that business, done fairly, should change the lives of all involved.' That includes, first and foremost, the producers whom Little Trove is helping to work out of poverty.

For fair trade to be genuine trade and not an exercise in charity, it is vital that it sells high-quality products and items that customers really want. So Little Trove seeks to give customers the *very best* ethical products their artisans can make. 'Our suppliers want to make amazing homeware and fashion products. They want to make products that will make your house look great and make you look even better. Great product quality and ethics shouldn't be a trade-off.'

The Christian approach to business is essentially one in which all relationships matter. We should treat everyone we encounter with care, dignity and respect, because each human being is made in God's image. All the entrepreneurs we interviewed sought to operate according to this fundamental principle. This includes the person or company one might be inclined to view as one's enemy – a business competitor. Love like this does not come easily, yet God enables and equips people to meet this formidable challenge. Jews and Samaritans did not get on, but in Jesus' parable the travelling Samaritan helped his fellow Jewish traveller who had been mugged by robbers. Christian entrepreneurs can set an example in showing love that is similarly universal.

10. 'WHO THEN IS THAT FAITHFUL AND WISE STEWARD?'

We have already argued that an important aspect of entre-preneurship is taking the lead in *marshalling resources*. This idea takes on an extra dimension for Christians. Resources are not ultimately a matter of human creation, nor ours to do what we like with. They are God-given, and we are accountable to God for our handling of them. This brings us to a key concept that featured in several interviews: stewardship.

One interviewee, Gavin Oldham, made a major separation between stewardship and enterprise. He is the founder of the Share Centre, Share Radio and the Share Foundation, which all seek to democratize wealth creation in order to address the challenges of economic inequality. He envisions a more egalitarian form of capitalism, where people have control over their lives, increased confidence in financial matters and opportunity to achieve their potential, through making direct share ownership more widely available to the ordinary public. The empowerment and respect for others which are integral to these aims are for Gavin a very important aspect of loving your neighbour.

When asked the question, 'Do you think local churches should consider making investment in small Christian businesses?' Gavin's answer was a straightforward *no*. He thinks the church, both on a local and national scale (he has served as a church commissioner), needs to invest money in a highly responsible way, not taking risks with other people's money. He contrasts this fiduciary duty with an entrepreneur's attitude to investment, where enterprise is rightly subject to considerable risks. For him stewardship is essentially about preserving what has been passed on intact, while enterprise is more creative.

Go forth and multiply

Most of the entrepreneurs we interviewed, however, saw things differently. They saw entrepreneurship as an expression of stewardship. For them the God-given command in Genesis 1:28 to 'be fruitful and multiply' applies not only to having children but to the whole human enterprise, including business. Matthew Kimpton-Smith talks about stewardship in terms of maximizing what God has given you. He applies this in a very personal way:

> God has made each one of us uniquely. As a person, as
> Matthew, I have been given certain skills. Some of these
> are physical skills, some mental, some interpersonal. God
> says, 'I knew you before you were born' (Jeremiah 1:5).
> I was made, he knows me, and he made me special.
> When you take on board the idea of being known in the
> womb, you realize that God has a special plan for you,
> a plan for you to follow. Of course we have the free will

to do things our own way, to curse, take drugs and blow our lungs. But we also have the opportunity to take what God has given us and maximize it.

Jody Wainwright has a similarly exuberant approach to stewardship. He says:

As Christians we have an opportunity to bring things into being. Everything about the Bible is increase and multiply. The parable of the talents says, 'What did you do with your talents? How did you invest what God has given you?' So it's about being excited and being practical. For me the process of being excited involves rallying together, using my enthusiasm to bring people in the business together for a vision. The Bible is full of multiplication: telling us to get out there, to multiply, to use our talents, to be more than conquerors. We can do it. Colossians 1 says that all things are held together through Christ. As he's holding everything together we can do something. He's not holding things together for us to play safe and nothing happens, so that we just coast along. Let's get out there!

Do you feel this way?

Eric Payne started and built up Mita Ltd, a company manu-facturing plastic conduit, trunking and cable containment systems which are sold throughout the world. He emphasizes the responsibility that humans have in extracting and refining the material resources that God has provided. This is a logical extension of the command to till and keep the garden in Genesis 2. Eric says:

God created a universe beyond our imagination. Here we are on planet Earth, and everything that we need for our life is either grown or it's mined. Think of any product, anything that we use, anything that we eat: it has been provided by God. It is there. If we want to make something out of steel, the iron ore is underground. If we want to make something out of plastic, we use oil that's in the ground; we refine and process it and use the by-products to make plastic raw materials. If we want to make something out of wood, the trees are growing. All the food we have is either plant life or animal life, which is grown. If we want to create energy, there is uranium in the ground that we can process into a nuclear reactor. Everything that's there is God-given, and that's no accident. God has also given us the ability to take these resources and use them, hopefully, for human good. Sadly, because of sin, they're often not used in the way that God intended. But they are there to be used – and could be used – for the blessing of the whole of humanity.

A sense of stewardship has different emphases for different people. For Simon Berry, Managing Director of a hotel group in north-west England, English Lakes Hotels Resorts & Venues, it relates to the essence of his company. 'My brother and I, who own the business, believe that fundamentally it's God's business, so we're custodians of God's business. If you like, he's the chairman, and we're his agents here looking after it for this time.' Simon's brother has not always been a Christian, but became one after they had worked together for seven years. To have a shared sense of running the business as God's business is very special to Simon. The two brothers recently won a Hotel and Leisure Family Business of the Year award, the group being praised for its approach to corporate social responsibility, green tourism, charitable work, creativity, innovation and commitment to staff development and training.

Money, time, family

Some people dislike the word 'stewardship'. It has negative connotations. For them it has an old-fashioned, dry and musty feel; they associate it with the business of fundraising, often done in a heavy-handed way. However, stewardship is not just about the handling of money. It does include our use of money, but extends much further than that. Stewardship embraces the whole of life.

For property developer Caroline, the realization that 'the Bible tells us to be good stewards of resources' *was* a wake-up call in terms of her handling of money. She says that her previous life as an air hostess encouraged her to love the world of glamour, which meant she had a certain lifestyle she felt she had to maintain.

> When I started the business my spending habits were still really bad. If you try to run a business and your spending habits are bad, you're going to go broke very quickly, because whatever comes in you want to spend. So I sat down with my mentor and he said to me: 'Where does your money go?' I began to learn where money should go every month. So rather than just having one bank account, I have many accounts. My mentor says: write down the seven areas where your money should go. When you spend money you're investing. So I either make a good investment or a bad investment. You go and buy a dress. Is it a good investment or a bad investment? My hair had been the most important thing in my life. I spent thousands just to get my hair done every week. I had to realize that was wasting money. So I identified money for investment, money for savings, money for my tithe, *some* money for my hair . . .

Caroline identified seven key areas of personal spending and apportioned an envelope for each. If the money ran out in any envelope, she accepted that she could not spend any more in that area that month. She learned that 'success is a few simple things you practise every day'. Caroline has applied this not just to her personal life but also to the business she runs.

Stewardship of time includes not being easily distracted. E-retailer Gareth exercises discipline in following the example of Nehemiah who, when enticed to a meeting, sent the reply: 'I am doing a great work and I cannot come down. Why should the work stop while I leave it?' (Nehemiah 6:3). In this case the distraction was coming from Jerusalem's enemies, Sanballat and Tobiah, who were conspiring to foil Nehemiah's God-given work. Distraction can also come from people who do not intend harm, but like to while away the hours and have the gift of the gab! There is a tension here, because entrepreneurs often pride themselves on their concern for people and readiness to make time for them. We need to be careful that they do not divert us from achieving our daily and weekly goals. Gareth observes:

> As somebody who is easily distracted and likes to get on to the next project, next conversation, something exciting, it's a discipline to say, 'Actually, I've got my work laid out, and I need to do it. It will suffer when I get involved in other things, so until I have completed that work or I'm released from that work, I focus!'

Car dealer Barry applies the notion of stewardship to the responsibility of bringing up children:

> I love the word stewardship. I think of our three young children as a gift from God that my wife and I have been

given to steward. We are their earthly parents, but they are gifts from God and we will steward them as best we can. So my understanding of stewardship is that everything in life is God's, and we are put in a position to tend, water and grow it as best as we can.

The reminder that this includes our children is very helpful.

The marshalling of resources entailed in stewardship does not always come easily. Sometimes we experience frustration: things just do not come together. Carpenter Peter experiences great job satisfaction when he is working with the grain of the wood, literally and metaphorically. 'But sometimes I'm wood fighting rather than wood working. I get frustrated with materials, time, energy and myself.' We have all had that experience. Sometimes we need to pause, collect ourselves, pray to God, reconsider our approach and make a fresh attempt to marshal resources effectively.

Garden parks and recycled carpets

In the present time, wise stewardship of God-given resources has assumed additional importance because of the current ecological crisis. The development of fossil fuels to power electricity has made possible major advances in our standard of living, but on a global level the benefits have not been shared equitably, and the use of fossil fuels has come at a massive cost to the environment. We need to reduce our emissions of methane and carbon dioxide, develop renewable sources of energy, and adopt a philosophy of recycling rather than constantly creating new material goods.

These necessities may put curbs on entrepreneurs, but they also create new opportunities for them. We have already cited individuals who are rising to this challenge. David Ball is pioneering the use of a low-carbon alternative to cement. Andrew Tanswell has produced for an African market panels, LED lamps and battery packs which harness solar power and combine high performance, affordability and durability.

Concern for the environment is also fundamental to Brian Clouston's work. He says:

> I don't think you can be a horticulturalist or a landscape designer without knowing that all we deal with is a gift from God, his creation. When you're designing, you're assisting with that creative process. It's a privilege to be involved in healing a damaged landscape. One project we worked on in Sunderland was a 182-acre site, a former coal waste tip that was actually on fire and red hot. I couldn't transform that into a park, a recreation area which now attracts two million visits a year, without being inspired to do it. I was very conscious throughout my career of being directed by the Lord. If I saw an opportunity I would simply ensure that I spoke to the right person, explained the idea and then tried to persuade them to implement it.

The 'right person' included politician Michael Heseltine when he was Minister for the Environment. Brian helped persuade him to hold five national garden festivals in the early 1990s. They involved the cultural regeneration of large tracts of derelict land in the industrial areas of Liverpool, Stoke-on-Trent, Glasgow, Gateshead and Ebbw Vale.

Simon Macaulay is Managing Director of Anglo Recycling, a family business situated in a 150-year-old cotton mill in the beautiful Rossendale Valley on the edge of the Pennines. Simon has been busy selling carpets since the late 1990s, when he took over the company from his father. 'I really wanted to carry on what my father had started. That was a very powerful motivation for me. I gave up a job paying twice as much as I could earn here, and Kate my wife agreed to move.' It was a big risk, but Simon has not regretted it.

During the 2000s the company struggled to make money, but towards the end of the decade they identified a possible niche market in the area of recycling. In 2010 Anglo installed a recycling plant. Using low-energy techniques and 100% recycled fibres, they now manufacture a wide variety of felts for the flooring, horticulture, building insulation and acoustic industries. Anglo has developed a technique which pulls the fibres from wool-rich carpet offcuts and produces a new carpet underlay, Reco. This diverts 600 tonnes of carpet from going to landfill. Their manufacturing methods combine traditional needle looms with the latest textile technologies. Anglo underlay has supplied several Hilton Hotels, as well as the Strand Palace.

Simon's company is an excellent example of sustainable business. His Christian faith inspires all he does. He employs a local Baptist minister as a company chaplain, a much appreciated ministry, and has set up a social enterprise offering work experience to young adults with special needs, many autistic.

Whatever the line of business an entrepreneur pursues, there are now ecological challenges which cannot be ignored. Every company should consider its carbon footprint, along with ways in which it can recycle more and waste less. For Christians it is an axiomatic part of being good stewards of God's creation.

Faithful and unfaithful servants

In all the talk about stewardship, one of Jesus' parables features frequently. Ironically, the two parables in which Jesus talks explicitly about stewards (Luke 12:42–48 and 16:1–9) receive less attention than one which does *not* use the word 'steward': the parable of the talents. Along with 'seek ye first the kingdom of God', this was the passage cited most often by our entrepreneurs as inspiring them. Interestingly, Gavin Oldham sees the parable of the talents as an encouragement to enterprise rather than stewardship.

The story is familiar: the master summons three servants and entrusts his property to them, giving one five talents, the second two and the third one. The first two go off, trade and double the number of talents they have. The third simply digs a hole in the ground and hides his master's money. When the master returns after a long time away, he is pleased with the first two servants and rewards them with further talents and responsibility, but he is angry with the third servant and denounces him as wicked and lazy.

This parable has provoked an enormous amount of debate. Some have seen it as justifying the practice of usury, because the master says to the third servant that at the very least 'you ought to have invested my money with the bankers, and on my return I would have received what was my own with interest' (Matthew 25:27). Others have recoiled against that interpretation, arguing that this is simply a detail of the story. A fashionable trend in recent liberation theology is to regard the third servant as the unlikely hero, because he has the courage to face up to the master and implicitly criticize him for 'reaping where you did not sow, and gathering where you did not scatter seed' (Matthew 25:24). He tells the rich man the truth about himself and refuses to collude with unrighteous money-making. The problem with this is that the interpreter ends up appearing to know better than Jesus himself, teaching something at variance with the received text. Although Jesus often sided with the poor and marginalized, that need not stop him on other occasions siding with the economically productive. The poor man in this parable brought poverty on himself by doing nothing with the one talent he had.

Unsurprisingly, the entrepreneurs we interviewed who cited this parable understand it in the more conventional way. They see it as commending the practice of trade and a productive use of money, or in a more general way as urging that we put our God-given skills to positive use. It is interesting how the word 'talent', which originally meant a large sum of money, has come to indicate an ability or skill. The point of the parable is that we maximize whatever we have been given in God's purposes. We have already seen how Jody seizes enthusiastically on the idea of 'multiplication'.

Our entrepreneurs varied, however, in the main message from the parable that they took to heart. Keith Noronha is convinced that 'if you hang on to the gifts God has given you, hide them in the ground and do nothing with them, that's a waste for the society you live in'. Keith is conscious of the fact that he received a good education, something his parents paid for, and 'my way of saying thank you to God is to do the best I can in business'.

Andrew Tanswell is struck by the fact that God issued exactly the same praise to both the servant with five talents and the servant with two: 'Well done, good and trustworthy slave; you have been trustworthy in a few things, I will put you in charge of many things; enter into the joy of your master' (Matthew 25:21, 23). The servant who made five more talents is not praised any more than the servant who made two more. Andrew comments: 'Not everybody has the same talents or an equal quota of talents. Not everyone is going to be the President of the United States, the Prime Minister, or Archbishop of the Church of England.' The question is whether we make the most of what skills we have been given.

Martin Clark is fascinated by the way that the parable of the talents is followed immediately by the parable of the sheep and the goats (Matthew 25:31–46). A story about success in trading precedes a story about having mercy on those who are hungry, thirsty, naked, sick or in prison. Martin believes that, taken together, the two parables give justification to the practice of social enterprise. One advocates an entrepreneurial attitude, the other encourages kindness and charity. Social enterprise – enterprise with the good of needy social groups in view – combines the two. Martin suggests it is the missing link, the 'glue' that binds the parables. That is an idea well worth considering.

In and under authority

Along with the models of servant and shepherd, which we looked at in chapter 9, the Bible presents steward as a third leadership image. However, steward is not a picture of outright leadership but more akin to middle management. The essence of a steward's position is that he or she is both in and under authority.

This comes out clearly in the parable Jesus told in Luke 12:42–48. He asks: 'Who then is that faithful and wise steward, whom his master will make ruler over his household, to give them their portion of food in due season?' (NKJV) The Greek word used here for 'steward' is *oikonomos*, from which we derive the word 'economics'. It denotes a household manager, someone who works in a large house under the master's authority but has considerable responsibility in terms of ordering food and other provisions for all the household members, family and servants. Described initially as a steward in verse 42, the same character is called a servant in verses 43 and 45. The *oikonomos* looks both ways: looking upwards to the master and being very much *under* authority, and looking downwards to the junior servants over whom he is decidedly *in* authority. It is the same status as the Roman centurion whom Jesus met in Luke 7:1–10. The centurion said: 'I also am a man set under authority, with soldiers under me; and I say to one, "Go", and he goes, and to another, "Come", and he comes, and to my slave, "Do this", and the slave does it.'

Christian entrepreneurs with a strong notion of steward-ship see their business in a similar way. Yes, they wield considerable authority over their employees, but they also regard themselves as accountable to God. God is the one to whom they are ultimately answerable. Matthew Turnour, senior partner in a law firm, speaks for many when he says: 'I try to be faithful to the call of God on my life, and to be a wise steward of the resources I have been given. I see the firm as one of the most important stewardship responsibilities I have and trust God for its outcomes.'

Where business leaders lack that sense of being under authority and accountability, the results can be frightening. Where someone is not under authority the contrast is a display of naked power. Naked, untrammelled power is the freedom and ability to do whatever one likes. In the Luke 12 parable, Jesus describes two scenarios. The first is the steward doing his job well and being praised by the master when he returns. The second is the steward abusing his power, beating the servants, overeating and getting drunk; he will then be severely punished by the master.

Entrepreneurs who own and run companies that have grown to a substantial size often find themselves in a position of naked power. In some ways they are more powerful than the chief executives of large public limited companies, because the latter have greater accountability both to their board of directors and to institutional shareholders. Entrepreneurs are subject to fewer constraints. One interviewee asserted: 'As the owner of the company I am in a unique position – in the end I make the rules. So I can make decisions that other Christians in business who are not at the same level of authority can't make.'

We agree. There are two particular areas where Christian entrepreneurs need to take care – especially those whose companies have grown large and they have become wealthy. One is the area of pay and salary structure. We were actually surprised that this did not emerge as more of an issue in the interviews. What do entrepreneurs pay themselves, and how do they decide what is an appropriate remuneration? What do they pay their workforce? At the lower level do they simply pay the minimum wage, the living wage or something better? We would hope that, in the cause of justice, firms run by Christian entrepreneurs have narrower wage differentials than most. This was clearly true of some companies covered in our survey.

The second and connected area concerns what entrepreneurs do with their money. It is tempting to follow the way of the world in terms of purchasing large houses, flashy cars and all the other material accompaniments which tend to go with position and power. If we make such purchases, do we then make these possessions widely available to others? There are certainly some entrepreneurs who have bought large houses and are generous in opening them up for use by other groups.

Isaiah 22 contains a challenging passage about a steward who had got too big for his boots:

> Thus says the Lord God of hosts: Come, go to this steward, to Shebna, who is master of the household, and say to him: 'What right do you have here? Who are your relatives here,

that you have cut out a tomb here for yourself, cutting a tomb
on the height, and carving a habitation for yourself in the
rock? The LORD is about to hurl you away violently, my fellow
. . . I will thrust you from your office, and you will be pulled
down from your post.
(Isaiah 22:15–19)

Of course, this does not mean that making a tomb in advance
of one's death is necessarily a bad thing. In the Gospels, the
rich man Joseph of Arimathea made a new tomb, hewn out
of the rock, but then offered its use for Jesus as an offering of
love when Jesus died before him (Matthew 27:57–59). Are we
ready to make our possessions available to others who are in
greater need?

Accountability

In making decisions about such matters, it is helpful for
Christian entrepreneurs to be accountable not just to God but
to a carefully chosen friend or group of friends. Most of our
entrepreneurs recognized that their work carried considerable
temptations in relation to money, power and status; there can
be sexual temptation, too, especially for those involved in
frequent business trips to far-off parts of the world. One said:
'Entrepreneurs must be part of an accountability structure,
especially an accountability partner.' This is a group or individual with whom they meet regularly to share, discuss and
to pray. For this to work, entrepreneurs need to commit to:

- making such meetings a priority;
- being ruthlessly honest;
- admitting when they have problems;
- a willingness to be challenged at a deep level.

We strongly commend being part of an accountability group.

One area where it is helpful to have peers who are a sounding-board is in the making of difficult moral decisions. This is the area of entrepreneurship to which we now turn.

11. AVOIDING SHARP AND DODGY PRACTICES

Without integrity, entrepreneurs can easily go haywire. This is a clear message that emerged from chapter 3. During the 1970s and 1980s, entrepreneurs suffered from a 'dodgy' image because several notable entrepreneurs – both real and fictional – lacked integrity. Qualities such as enthusiasm, energy, creativity, innovation and a willingness to take risks are all very well, but they can be harnessed to evil ends. Entrepreneurship has a negative side. Some entrepreneurs are greedy; some have inflated egos; some are dangerous visionaries. They may be impatient about achieving their goals, taking moral short cuts, being prepared to do whatever it takes to make their business successful. They may be ruthless in their methods to eliminate the competition. If entrepreneurs are to be godly people who contribute to the good of society, they need integrity.

Several interviewees felt integrity was what distinguished them as Christian entrepreneurs. With due humility, they felt they had earned a reputation for integrity which made others want to do business with them.

You may wonder why integrity should be the moral virtue emphasized above others. The Bible, after all, has more to say about love and justice than integrity. In *Ethics and Excellence*, American author Robert Solomon gives a persuasive answer: 'Integrity is not so much a virtue itself as it is a complex of virtues, the virtues working together to form a coherent character, an identifiable and trustworthy personality.' Integrity suggests, logically enough, a life that is well integrated. There is a coherence between the different parts. The value system professed is adhered to in all areas of life, public and private.

Paying taxes

Is there anything we can learn from Jesus about integrity? Yes.

In Mark 12:13, Jesus' opponents come to him and say, 'Teacher, we know that you are a man of integrity' (NIV). The Greek reads literally 'we know that you are sincere or truthful'. You are not swayed by others; you pay no attention to who they are. In other words, Jesus, you are not a person-pleaser; you do not give in to peer pressure; you teach the way of God in accordance with the truth. These words are hugely ironic, because they are said by Jesus' opponents in order to flatter him, with the aim of trapping him. But they are profoundly true. The Pharisees could not have been more accurate in describing Jesus' way of working, his style of speaking.

There is integrity too in how Jesus replies. The trick question about whether to pay taxes to Caesar was designed to catch Jesus out. Either Jesus would alienate the crowds by uncritically supporting the payment of taxes, or he would denounce the tax and get into trouble with the Roman authorities. He refuses to be trapped. Instead he articulates a dual allegiance. He asks for a coin to be brought to him, inquires whose image and inscription are on it, and then utters the famous words: 'Give to Caesar the things that are Caesar's, and to God the things that are God's.'

'Give to Caesar what is Caesar's.' The probable force of this is: if Caesar has his head on the coin, let him have it back. It belongs to him. But the emphasis of Jesus' reply lies in the second part: 'Give to God what is God's.' Our lives, which bear God's image, belong to God. The challenge for Christian entrepreneurs is to give their lives to God. This is the punchline which left Jesus' opponents awestruck.

Jesus' reply is often misunderstood. He is not demarcating two distinct areas of life, one labelled 'politics' and the other labelled 'religion' – two compartments with a strong dividing line down the middle. It is more like two concentric circles, one larger than the other. What is owed to Caesar is contained *within* what is owed to God. Yes, there are legitimate duties we owe to secular authority, whether that is the authority of a company or the authority of government. Normally these include the payment of taxes. But these need to be considered in the light of our ultimate allegiance to God.

Paying taxes fully was an issue mentioned by several of our entrepreneurs in answer to the question: 'Do you think there are some sharp or dodgy practices, which are a particular temptation for entrepreneurs in the pursuit of wealth?' Hotel manager Simon Berry put this in the wider context of money management:

The enemy will test us and tempt us wherever we are weak, wherever he perceives a weakness, and the area that is most likely to get the entrepreneur is money management. That could be not running your tax affairs correctly, not handling your accounts correctly, or not paying suppliers on time and in a right fashion – not because you want more money but because you get yourself into a cash-flow problem. You think, 'So, things are a bit tight. Well, let's just delay the payments a bit and if we fill in the tax return a certain way we can save a bit of money.' That's not paying Caesar what is Caesar's due.

Bolstered by his accountant's advice, Gareth has resolved to avoid tax avoidance as well as tax evasion:

The practice of handling taxes is the issue I have seen at the forefront for other businesspeople. I was on a university course for a few years, and met a group of business owners whose preoccupation was how to avoid paying taxes. I have an accountant who is a Christian; appointing him was a deliberate decision. I said to him, 'These are ideas they've suggested; this is what so-and-so is doing. What should we do?' He said, 'Do what you are already doing, don't change anything: make no use of taxes or loopholes to avoid paying into society.'

David Bishop is a dentist who runs his own practice. Like many others, he experiences pressure to connive with other tradespeople in not declaring *their* tax. He says:

When you're running a business you have to employ people to do the plumbing, the electricity and all the rest of it. So supposing you need a new gas boiler, you get someone in to give you a quote and they say: 'OK, that will be £1,000, but only £800 for cash.' It's a big temptation to think. 'OK, I could use the cash I've saved.' But is that the right thing? You wouldn't be rendering to Caesar what is Caesar's. It also works the other way. I've given patients a quote for some treatment, and they say, 'OK, but what's the real figure if I give you cash? How much discount would I get?' That's a temptation, but I've always felt able to resist it. I say, 'That's the price, however you pay me.'

Mark Mitchell stressed the complexity of tax requirements and the need to view them in the current political context:

> Different countries have different tax regimes, and the current climate in the UK is generally good for entrepreneurs. But you've got to be careful as a Christian that you're whiter than white. In the UK, companies have a number of regular visits from a number of different agencies: the VAT, Customs and Excise, Pay As You Earn, Income Tax, Corporation Tax, and then the business rates we pay to local government. They all speak to one another. So if you step out of line, three or four different agencies will find out. As well as me knowing it's the wrong thing to do, common sense in entrepreneurial life now says you need to stay on the right side of the law. And of course, if we want our hospitals open and our street lights on, we need to be making our contribution and paying our taxes.

Echoing this last point, film-maker Jeremy Higham practises and advocates a positive attitude towards paying taxes:

> I feel God shows us that we are to be bold, generous and honest tax payers. We should be cheerful givers to our nation, not reluctant givers who structure our affairs to minimize our tax. We should be bold and confident givers, who seek to lead the way and model generosity to our country and those in our country who benefit most from donations. We should let the Inland Revenue be our guide, but feel free to give more than they ask for.

This positive and cheerful attitude to paying tax is unusual, refreshing and – we have to admit – challenging.

Let's return to the subject of Jesus and integrity. Although the word may occur infrequently, we believe it is consistently present in Jesus' actions. There was real integrity, for instance, about the way Jesus entered Jerusalem on Palm Sunday. Jesus could just have walked into Jerusalem, as he doubtless had on several previous visits. But he chose not to – he decided to *ride* in. The way he entered Jerusalem was an important statement about his identity. Riding was a way of showing he was a king. But notice what sort of animal he rode. If he had been the conventional military messiah that many of his followers wanted him to be, he would have ridden on a horse. By choosing to enter on a donkey, he was communicating a different message. He was fulfilling the prophecy of Zechariah 9:9: 'Lo, your king comes to you; triumphant and victorious is he, humble and riding on a donkey.' Jesus was coming in peace, not stirring up war. But he was still ready to accept the acclamation of the crowds.

Jesus' entry had integrity. For business leaders today, choice of the right sort of symbolic actions can often say a great deal about their character. We believe that Simon Lawson's practice of cooking lunch for his employees strikes an admirable note. For an entrepreneur who lacks the gift of cooking, however, it would be less appropriate! We need to find symbolic actions that are true to us, that convey our character but also God's character.

Improper payments

The word 'integrity' also appears in the Old Testament, most often in the books that scholars call the wisdom literature – Psalms, Proverbs and Job. In Psalm 26 the writer twice talks about 'walking in my integrity' (26:1, 11). This contrasts with people 'in whose hands are evil devices, and whose right hands are full of bribes' (26:10). When the Old Testament mentions integrity and righteousness, the issue of bribery is never far away. In Psalm 15, the description of the righteous people who walk 'blamelessly' (15:2) includes the fact that they 'do not take a bribe against the innocent' (15:5).

Richard has analysed the biblical material on bribery in *Faith, Hope and the Global Economy*. He concludes that the main reason the Bible condemns bribes is because they result in a *perversion of judgment*. The lure of personal gain sways decisions that should be made on impartial grounds. Bribery violates standards of public service. It is a betrayal of trust.

Most of the references in the Old Testament are judicial. The prophets in particular were concerned that accepting bribes would pervert a judge's judgment, so that the guilty (often the rich) were acquitted or the innocent (usually the poor) convicted. The judge's capacity to weigh the evidence objectively would be jeopardized. In the case of a government minister or civil servant assessing the merits of rival corporate tenders, there is a similar need for cool impartiality. Justice is a key concept in business, though it tends to be relegated behind considerations of utility.

Several of the entrepreneurs we interviewed mentioned bribes, or 'improper payments', as a pervasive issue with which they grappled, often when dealing with particular parts of the world such as the Middle East, the Far East and Africa. Some had developed a stern and unwavering stance on the issue.

David Ball, for instance, said he had 'avoided sharp or dodgy practices from day one'. He gave two examples where he had come under strong pressure to forgo his integrity. The first was when the company's distributor in the Middle East tried to charge the end user nearly twice the figure quoted by the Cambridge manufacturer. A letter of credit was suggested with the inflated amount rather than the lower, original quotation, and this was justified on the grounds that 'This is how we do business in Arab countries. Part of the money will go to my elderly mother who lives in the States. Part of it goes to the man who's placing the order with me.' David recalled, 'I told the distributor that he would have to place the business elsewhere.'

The second instance was a contract where a negotiator asked outright for a large sum of money. David commented:

> Normally what happens in the Middle East is that a senior contract manager gives you the contract and if it was coming up to Christmas or maybe the baptism of his child you would buy something like a little special gold bracelet – maybe costing £40 or £50. This project manager asked outright, 'What's in this for me?', indicating that he expected to receive a substantial, personal financial sum in return for placing the order. Within a month he was on his way home.

Matthew Kimpton-Smith described a difficult situation out in the Far East, when discussing a possible project.

> A company owner said to me, 'I trust you're taking care of the project manager.' I said, 'What do you mean?' He said, 'This guy is sixty-two. He has worked in the family since the age of twelve. He has no education and is dependent on his salary. He's very proud and we can't give him his money. So his retirement is his project. We allow for the fact that all machine builders will give him a percentage of the contract value because that's his pension. If he doesn't get that he can't talk to you. I mean he has worked for us all this time and this is our gift to him. So you need to take care of him.'

Matthew was struck by the very different corporate attitude evident in another culture. Here was a company that was systematically devolving its responsibility for employees' pension provision to other companies with which it did business. In the end the project never happened.

Adrian was open in describing the complexities of doing business in the Far East. He said:

> We have never been asked: 'Please pay X amount and if you pay it we will guarantee the order.' We've never been put in that position. We have never offered a bribe. What does happen is that you are asked: 'Can you reduce your price? If you can match this price you can get the order . . .' Sometimes you know very well that the company you are selling to needs to sell at a higher margin. They need to make a substantial profit because from that profit they need to pay somebody.

Adrian continued:

> Singapore and Hong Kong, our two key markets, are relatively corruption-free compared to other markets in the Far East. There are usually quite strict controls on corrupt practices in Hong Kong and Singapore. The way they get around this is that a lot of entertaining takes place at senior levels. It's about giving them lifestyle benefits rather than a brown envelope of dollars slipped under the table. We have been taken out for dinner where senior architects and consultants are being entertained expensively by one of our customers. Somebody has to pay for that and the only way to pay is by putting higher margins on the product.

Adrian said that another problem is the pressure to describe products on documents as different from what they are. 'Yes, we have done that on occasions. It can create problems. It depends on what you are selling and who you are selling it to.'

He sees a need to circumvent national legislative regulations when they make little sense.

> In one country, for example, you are not allowed to export fire detection sirens because they require a police permit, and you're not meant to sell anything to that country that sounds like a police car, while the customs and excise say you can't import them without a licence for a major project. Yet these things are needed by the oil and gas industry for very strong safety reasons. The regulations say you have to have these safety devices offshore, but the customs and excise say you can't import them. What do you do? Describe it as something completely different.

This is a difficult situation. The response of Adrian's firm, though far from ideal, is understandable. If such practice is to be justified, it should not be done on a weakly pragmatic basis of 'the end justifies the means'. Rather it should be seen in terms of prioritizing one moral duty (to improve safety, which is what sirens do) above another which normally holds sway (to be transparent in corporate documentation). Do you face any moral dilemmas which are similar in type?

Two entrepreneurs reflected on the challenge of doing business without corruption in Africa. Grant Smith said:

> I would like to say we have never paid bribes, but the ability to be completely straight in business and be successful can almost only be done in God's strength. I actually think most business has a corrupt twisted side. It's the same in Britain; it's just a little more subtle than it is in Kenya.

Another entrepreneur made a similar point. He complained about the high costs of paying for goods to be kept in containers in the customs of a Western country, awaiting X-ray inspection:

> The reason the costs are so high – thousands of dollars – is that one company has the monopoly for the whole custom X-ray system, and the reason they get a monopoly is that they give millions of dollars to a political campaign. If that happened in Africa you would simply say that's government bribery.

Phil Schluter could give examples from Africa where he had been asked for an outright bribe. At one airport in central Africa a military commander with a gun around his neck told Phil that his visa was not valid. Phil had actually spent a week's time and 'I don't know how much money' to get this visa from the relevant embassy in London. His passport was temporarily taken away. Eventually the situation was resolved. A similar problem happened in another country where permission to get a licence was dependent on a consultant paying the relevant government minister $2,000. Phil is adamant that he has 'never paid a bribe in Africa. You have to trust God to see you through a situation, even though an unwillingness to pay often means you have to sit and wait a long time.'

What this and other examples illustrate is that there is often a cost attached to integrity. Practising high standards of business ethics is easy and straightforward when doing the right thing incurs no financial disadvantage. But if it loses you business, if it means you fail to win a contract or you wait for several months to progress your business, integrity becomes much more testing. Being a faithful follower of Jesus in business may require that sacrifice.

Honesty in marketing

For some people, integrity and honesty are virtually syn-
onymous. We believe integrity is a larger concept of which
honesty is a part, but it is a very important part.

An ethical conundrum mentioned by several entrepreneurs
was honesty in sales and marketing. This is perhaps less clear
cut than many issues in business, but is real nonetheless.

Martin Clark summed the temptation up as 'exaggeration'.
Others might call it 'puffery'.

> You're trying to show how successful you are. When you're
> applying for funding you tend to put a positive spin. I think
> that's probably normal and within the bounds of reasonable
> ethics. But when it gets to the point where you exaggerate,
> cover up failures and – even more – pretend that you're more
> successful than you are, because you need to do so to win
> some funding, that's a problem.

Some entrepreneurs located the problem among staff:

- 'You need to get Christian values into sales people.
  They're on commission, so they will instigate some
  of the dodgy practices.'
- 'Telling lies is an endemic problem. Often it's tempting
  to say as a buyer your competitors come in at a pound,
  when in fact the competitor's price is £1.10.'

Temptation, however, can afflict us all. We may be so keen
to trumpet the virtues of our product that we play down its
drawbacks or present a misleading picture. It might involve
pretending that a product is ready and waiting to be delivered
before that is true: what one entrepreneur called 'selling

things that aren't 100% there yet'. Is this something you wrestle with?

Mike Clargo thinks that 'the promotional aspects of marketing are potentially a shabby practice. That overstates it a bit but the purpose of a lot of advertising seems to be creating dissatisfaction. You're wanting to make people less content with what they've got, in order to move them towards something you want them to have.'

The area of marketing, especially advertising, is replete with potential problems. These include exaggeration (inflated claims), manipulation (working on people's unconscious associations) and promotion of superficial image (appealing to pride and status). Yet marketing can be practised in an ethical way. If the goods or services being sold by a company carry genuine merit, there is nothing wrong with telling the world about them. Marketing is an exercise in mass communications, making the public aware of the life-enhancing product that an entrepreneur has to offer. The best sort of marketing consists of a sincere appreciation and affirmation of the product's benefits. This need not be po-faced: there is a place for humour and colour in marketing. Exaggeration needs to be distinguished from hyperbole that no-one is in danger of believing, such as Heineken's claim that it reaches parts of the body other beers do not. Nobody is in danger of taking that seriously. In contrast, claims that a car has passed safety checks or met environmental standards when it has not are seriously misleading, and therefore wrong.

Transparency

A good test of corporate honesty is what entrepreneurs do when things go wrong. When we make mistakes that are embarrassing, inconvenient or even endanger the public, the instinctive response is to deny, cover up or blame somebody else. That is not the response of someone with integrity. Where others might seek to cover their tracks, the integrity response is to be as transparent as possible.

Andrew Glover is Chief Executive and co-founder of the Cambridge IT firm Bridge Partners, which has now 'birthed' a second company, Bridge Fibres. Both have a turnover of about £1.5 million. Their website proclaims that they provide 'seamless IT support from hands-on help to high-level strategy', and most of the time this is exactly what they do provide. They have successfully established internet connectivity to many far-flung and previously unconnected parts of the Fenlands in East Anglia. However, Andrew recalls an incident when all Bridge Partners' customers lost their internet connection:

> It probably affected 150 or 200 companies and happened in the middle of the day. It was our fault: we had made a mistake, rather than it being *force majeure*, an unavoidable accident. We had to take the decision on how to respond, how to let people know what to do. Bizarrely, at the time I was taking a day off and was on an executive toolbox course run by the London Institute for Contemporary Christianity. But this worked out well because I was able to turn to other people and ask their advice. I was in the best possible environment for dealing with the problem.

Andrew's real-life dilemma became a group case study. This is how he responded.

> I emailed all our customers, taking time out during a lunch break. We were honest about why the incident had occurred and what we were doing about it. We apologized and made

restitution. We didn't lose any customers. A lot of people didn't say anything, but several came back to us and said that was really refreshing – no-one normally admits these things, so thank you for owning up. It's great to work with people who do that.

Bridge Partners acted with integrity, what Andrew calls 'the character trait of relationships'. He says:

I have always wanted to do business like that, in an open, honest way. The challenge is that you could equivocate, you could bend the truth a little bit, you could say we won't say anything because then we're not lying. But that wouldn't feel right.

Note too the significance of Andrew asking for advice in the moment of crisis. He found himself among fellow Christians in equivalent positions who confirmed his own moral instincts. 'Where there is no guidance, a nation falls, but in an abundance of counsellors there is safety' (Proverbs 11:14). God supplied Andrew with an abundance of counsellors when he most needed them!

In chapter 8 we introduced Phil Staunton, whose firm D2M works with other companies to develop new products. This requires trust on the customers' part as well as integrity on Phil's. He says: 'Interestingly, some clients find it very odd that we will be honest with them. They wonder why. They think it would make more sense for me to say "your idea's brilliant" and then pinch it to make money.' But D2M has won a reputation for integrity, so Phil is able to convince his clients that he really has their best interests at heart.

An important aspect of honesty for Phil is being frank with potential clients about whether their proposed product is commercially viable. This can be painful, because delivering a judgment that it is not viable may amount to shattering the client's dreams. However, it is important to have the courage to be honest: otherwise expectations may be falsely raised and valuable resources wasted. Phil has also learnt the importance of honesty in fully charging the client for work that D2M does for them; in the past he often underestimated the hours spent on projects.

No gambling, no pornography

Taking a moral stand may take the form of having nothing to do with a product which is regarded as having a damaging effect on people's lives.

Gordon Haynes described a situation where his company was offering a warehousing facility, on a site where he was not based himself. One of his salesmen did a deal with what he told Gordon was an electronics company.

> It was a very big deal. They would have been our biggest customer, but it turned out that what they wanted to store were gambling machines. The rest of my family are Christians and when they heard about it they said, 'Dad, what are you doing taking that in?' This stirred my conscience. So I wrote to the customer and said, 'I am sorry, but we can't house your products. Can you kindly remove them? I am a Christian and know many people who've had their lives damaged by gambling. I'm afraid I can't allow your goods on our premises.' When they wrote back I expected a scathing response, but that's not what I received. They said, 'Thank you for contacting us. We appreciate your view; we don't agree with it but we respect it and will withdraw our goods.' So we extracted ourselves from that situation satisfactorily. And we managed to fill the space in the warehouse.

A similar stand was taken by Daniel Cooper, an entrepreneur who works in media developing online technology. He became Chief Technology Officer of a company invested in by a major international media and electronics company. When the Chief Executive Officer moved on, Daniel became acting CEO. He explains:

> During that time I had the technology, marketing and sales teams reporting in to me. Once a salesman came into the office after a customer meeting, declaring, 'I've got this fantastic opportunity worth millions of dollars. It's with a major international player. They want all of their content to be moved online and interactive.' The company was a well-known adult magazine. So I considered some options. Either I could sweep this opportunity under the carpet and make it so expensive, so difficult, on such a long timescale that the magazine would never accept us as a supplier. Or I could say, 'We're not going to do this because of my beliefs as a Christian.'

Daniel chose the second option and raised the issue at a board meeting.

> I explained my Christian beliefs and the conflict with the opportunity, and finished by saying if they wanted to go for the business I would resign. My intent was not to 'hold a gun to anyone's head', but to make it clear I wouldn't compromise.

There was significant debate and many challenging questions. Daniel was only able to be persuasive because he did his best to understand and address alternative viewpoints. He managed to keep his calm, being strongly motivated by the desire to be 'salt and light' (Matthew 5:13–16). In the end he had the satisfaction of seeing his viewpoint triumph.

At home with the family

Gordon's experience shows that taking a moral stand is not necessarily costly in business. There are situations where we might anticipate financial loss, but in the providence of God this does not actually happen. Seeking God's kingdom and his righteousness, we find that material things are 'added as well' (Matthew 6:33).

This is certainly the testimony of the entrepreneurs who have taken a principled stand on Sunday trading. They are keen to cite God's words to Eli the priest in this connection: 'those who honour me I will honour' (1 Samuel 2:30). We have already referred in chapter 1 to the decisions made by Gary Grant and Mark Mitchell not to open their retail outlets on Sundays.

In neither case was it a particularly difficult decision. When Gary started The Entertainer, Sunday trading was not allowed, so it was a case of continuing as he was when the Sunday trading laws were relaxed. Mark came under pressure when Mitsubishi stipulated that their dealers should be open on Sundays, but was clear that it would be inconsistent for him to have his Mitsubishi business open while his Lexus business was closed.

One reason why Gary and Mark have been able to buck the trend and stay successful seems to be that they and their staff work exceptionally hard during the rest of the week. They offer outstanding customer care, and the public respect the stance they have taken and are happy to throng their aisles Monday to Saturday. The revenue that accrues six days a week more than compensates for what they forgo on the seventh day. Significantly, the Old Testament command to hallow the Sabbath day also says, 'Six days you shall labour and do all your work' (Exodus 20:9).

Note that these two entrepreneurs avoid a narrow sabbatarian stance on this issue. It is not a case of 'the word of God forbids this, so we won't do it'. Instead, they promote their position in a positive way, as a mark of their care for individuals and families. They want employees to be sure of having a day off each week. There is a biblical basis to this, because a rest from work is seen as crucial for human welfare. Jesus refrained from taking a legalistic approach to the Sabbath, but he did believe 'the sabbath was made for humankind' (Mark 2:27). Christian entrepreneurs who enable families to be together on Sundays are showing respect for that principle.

Consistency

Along with honesty and transparency, consistency is an important part of what it means to be a person of integrity. Leaders who are consistent do not surprise too many people with their moral decisions. Having set out their stall, they stick by it.

However, being consistent need not mean being boring and predictable. Think again of Jesus. In the Gospels we see him interacting with a series of very different individuals. Consider his encounters with Nicodemus, the Samaritan woman, the rich young ruler, the woman with the issue of blood, Zacchaeus and many others. No two incidents are the same. Yes, Jesus had an underlying view of humanity which is reflected in all these incidents: he saw human beings as sinners in need of forgiveness and people who were recipients of God's forgiveness. But Jesus has a specially tailored response that meets each particular situation. Some responses must have seemed surprising at the time, yet there is an integrity about them based on his relationship with God, his understanding of the kingdom of

God and his unique insight into the needs and longings of each individual.

May God help us all to live lives of integrity which mirror the life of Jesus, grounded on a close and vibrant relationship with God such as Jesus enjoyed himself – a relationship that helps us to make excellent decisions when the pressure is on.

12. TOO BUSY NOT TO PRAY

O God, you are my God, I seek you,
    my soul thirsts for you;
my flesh faints for you,
    as in a dry and weary land where there is no water.
So I have looked upon you in the sanctuary,
    beholding your power and glory.
Because your steadfast love is better than life,
    my lips will praise you.
So I will bless you as long as you live;
    I will lift up my hands and call on your name.
(Psalm 63:1–4)

We have chosen this psalm to begin a chapter on prayer because it focuses attention so clearly on God himself. When thinking of prayer in the context of work, it is easy for entrepreneurs to move swiftly into the area of requests: God help me, God give me strength, God determine a favourable outcome. There is a place for that sort of prayer, and we shall consider it shortly – but we must never fall into the trap of using God simply as a means to our ends. The psalms help us to appreciate God for the great God that he is, and to do so without rush. 'Because your steadfast love is better than life, my lips will praise you.' It is always good to start a time of prayer with praise and adoration.

Entrepreneurs pray more than most

A Baylor University study discovered that American entrepreneurs pray more than most people. Over half the entrepreneurs interviewed prayed daily, and a third several times a day. The researchers think this is because of the uncertainty entrepreneurs constantly face – hence the request for guidance or resolve. Prayer is one of the things that distinguishes Christian entrepreneurs from other entrepreneurs. They know they are not self-sufficient. They need the help of one greater than themselves.

Many of the entrepreneurs we interviewed affirmed the importance of prayer in their lives. This is a sample of their responses:

- 'It underlies everything. If I believe in my heart that this is God's business, I need a communication system that's established and right with him. That revolves around prayer.'
- 'I need to offer my enterprises and ideas first to God before embarking on them, and then continually offer them in prayer, especially when entering unknown territory.'
- 'Prayer is a vital part of my life. Going without prayer is like going out naked. I feel it's a huge part of me. It's a lifestyle.'

- 'Very important. We regularly commit our business to God. It's like Aaron invoking the Lord's blessing' (see Numbers 6:24–26).

Teach us to pray

Praying, however, does not come easily to many of us. Jesus' own disciples were conscious of being novices in this respect. They came to Jesus and said: 'Lord, teach us to pray' (Luke 11:1). Note that the disciples did not say 'teach us to preach' or 'teach us to heal', but 'teach us to pray'. They discerned that it was central to Jesus' way of life. His response was to teach them the Lord's Prayer, which provides a model prayer, one we can use both as it stands and as a structure for more detailed prayer.

Our entrepreneurs similarly discerned the priority of prayer and its fundamental importance in nurturing their relationship with God. But some of them struggled with its practice. They felt that they did not pray as much as they should or would like to. One said: 'I believe in prayer passionately and don't do anywhere near enough.' Two of them admitted to praying only sporadically or having no regular routine. Some serious obstacles to prayer among entrepreneurs emerged.

The busyness of their lives: This crowds out communication with God. One said: 'When I do pray, I'll be honest. I often end up falling asleep, because I am on the go all the time.' Another said: 'For busy guys finding time to pray is always going to be a challenge.' We sympathize: owning and running a business makes for a fearfully busy life. The challenge is compounded during stages of life when young children or aged parents make huge personal demands. But somehow most of us make time for things that we really value. Is prayer any different? John Wesley took the attitude that the busier he was, the more he needed to pray. His normal practice was to rise at 4 am and spend two hours in concentrated prayer. In order to make sure he had enough sleep, he disciplined himself by going to bed at 10 pm every night. Perhaps we can learn from his example.

Distraction: Some start to pray and then find their thoughts wandering off. One said: 'Quite often I head into work meaning to pray on the journey, but I start thinking about different people and the situations they're involved in. I find prayer difficult because it requires concentration.' One remedy for this is articulating prayers out loud. There is a place for silent prayer, but it can leave our minds more vulnerable to wander. Praying aloud keeps minds focused; it can also give prayer shape and purpose. One entrepreneur said: 'I like making quite a bit of noise when I pray.'

Spiritual battle: This is evident in the two obstacles just cited – busyness and distraction. Jody said: 'Prayer is the most important thing in my life. It's the most challenged thing as well. The enemy doesn't like it when we pray, because things happen.' How true that is! We should not be surprised if prayer is a struggle, because it is a spiritual battleground. The great passage in Ephesians 6 about putting on the whole armour of God ends: 'Pray in the Spirit at all times in every prayer and supplication' (Ephesians 6:18). Because prayer is hard work, we need the Holy Spirit's help. In Romans 8, Paul talks about prayer in the context of groaning. We groan and the Spirit groans on our behalf: 'Likewise the Spirit helps us in our weakness; for we do not know how to pray as we ought, but that very Spirit intercedes with sighs too deep for words' (Romans 8:26).

Unanswered prayer?

'I pray more because I know it's part of the walk that I'm supposed to take, rather than because I'm 100% confident it will deliver what I'm asking for.' Another reason why some Christians find prayer difficult is that they experience prayer that goes apparently unanswered. One entrepreneur who is going through a difficult phase with his business, whose key product is not taking off in the way that he hoped (despite frequent prayers to that effect), admitted his confusion. Another entrepreneur said this:

> I used to say help prayers a lot but I found it emotionally
> exhausting. If I have a problem, I find it better to stay calm
> and use my mind to work out an answer to the problem.
> Prayer is still important to me, but I use it to give peace
> and clarity of mind rather than look for quick-fix solutions.

Using one's God-given mind was also stressed by someone who made a distinction between praying for people and praying for situations. He said: 'I regularly pray for people in this workplace. I find it harder to pray for situations because I think I can solve situations. I think I can fix situations, but that's probably a weakness.'

There were other entrepreneurs who had joyful stories of answered prayer. Simon Macaulay of Anglo Recycling described this incident:

> A few years ago we had an awful three-month period and we
> lost £40,000 on a sale of £380,000, so we made over a 10%
> loss. The figures had been going down and down and we
> were in the middle of a recession. I thought, 'I can't turn this
> around.' I sat down with David, our company chaplain, and

we prayed together. I had a meeting next day with B&Q, and I had to ask them for a 23% price increase. David prayed that the guy I was going to see would be sympathetic and understanding. I felt that was a really key moment, because if I asked for an increase and B&Q turned me down, the business would be on a downward cycle. I went in and said to the buyer, 'I need a really big price increase.' To my surprise, he didn't fall off his chair. He told me that my main competitor had been in the week before and had asked for a 24% price increase! So we got the deal.

Simon took this to mean that 'God was there, and God wanted me to continue'. Simon's natural inclination is to worry, but he is learning to trust Jesus' words: 'Do not worry about your life' (Matthew 6:25).

Discernment and boldness

The issue of answered and unanswered prayer is complex. Yes, God has given us brains to work out sensible courses of action and we do not need to consciously pray over every small decision. When God does not appear to be answering our prayers in terms of desired business outcomes, it is worth asking whether we are pursuing the right route. Have we judged the market accurately? Is there something about our product or service that is proving a damaging Achilles heel? In such circumstances, it is well worth talking the situation through with business peers who will offer honest advice. This may give us greater discernment.

Sometimes God's answer to prayer is neither *yes* nor *no*, but *wait* – and *keep working*. He may be testing our determination and faithfulness. This is a theme we explore in the next chapter on perseverance. It is also possible God may have a *better plan*, and the apparently unanswered prayer can be a spur to finding it.

Phil Staunton prays every Monday morning with a group of friends who are all business leaders. He believes that 'the impact it has had on our businesses is both immeasurable and tangible'. Concerted prayer appears to have turned round the fortunes of a friend's business that had been going nowhere.

Jesus certainly encouraged us to be bold in our prayer requests: 'Ask, and it will be given you; search, and you will find; knock, and the door will be opened for you. For everyone who asks receives, and everyone who searches finds, and for everyone who knocks, the door will be opened' (Matthew 7:7–8). He compared God to a person answering his friend's request for bread even in the middle of the night (Luke 11:5–10). Richard and Kina can testify to many answered prayers in relation to Faith in Business. After careful discussion, we have prayed some very specific prayers about events, numbers attending events and financial needs. Our prayers have always stretched our faith; the outcomes we have sought have exceeded what we might reasonably have expected to happen anyway. In our experience, God has been consistently faithful.

Our testimony also confirms the value of praying with someone else. This adds fervency to our prayers; the faith of one inspires the other. Along with Phil, several more entrepreneurs spoke of the benefit they derive from praying with others. In some cases, it is a network of Christian business-people in comparable positions, meeting on a regular weekly or monthly basis. In other cases, it is the entrepreneur's spouse – especially where husband and wife are involved together in the business. For young entrepreneurs Natasha and her business partner Lavinia, it is their mothers who pray 'almost every day for us down the phone'. For another, serious prayer for the business takes place in that person's weekly home group. Where a company has the character of a 'Christian business', with a substantial number of the employees being Christians, the working week often begins with a prayer meeting and a collective offering of current issues and forthcoming events to God.

Forms of prayer

The forms of prayer that entrepreneurs use vary widely, just as is true of Christians in general.

Where individuals admitted operating without a set time of prayer, it was certainly not the case that they did not pray at all. This group tended to pray 'on the hoof'. One entrepreneur spoke of 'cues and reminders, triggers to help prayer. If I've got a meeting coming up and I go to make a cup of tea, I use the coffee machine or the toilet as the trigger. That's the point where I pray and ask God for wisdom to make the right decision.'

Consultant David Henderson spoke enthusiastically about *arrow prayers*:

> When somebody walks into the office and says, 'I've got a problem,' that's the time I would put a prayer up and say, 'Please help me to hear and guide whatever way is appropriate in the situation.' I find arrow prayers when you're in the middle of things immensely powerful.

Similarly, dentist David Bishop used arrow prayers when confronted by a tricky medical problem: 'God, please help me now!' A good example of arrow prayer in Scripture is Nehemiah 2:4. Nehemiah was in the presence of King Artaxerxes, who asked him, 'What do you request?' Nehemiah 'prayed to the God of heaven' – presumably a swift, very direct prayer – before he made his momentous request asking for permission to return to Jerusalem to rebuild it.

There is certainly a very important place for praying right in the midst of our workplaces, when the pressures are at their most intense. Billy Graham says: 'Remember you can pray anytime, anywhere. Washing dishes, digging ditches, working in the office, in the shop, on the athletic field, even in prison – you can pray and God hears.' Prayer is the living out of our relationship with God. We talk to God about the details of our business because we believe and know he cares about them.

Some entrepreneurs use their journeys to and from work as opportunities for conversation with God. For Gareth, prayer takes place

> between home, which is chaotic with small children getting ready for school, and stopping in the office car park. I then stop for 15 minutes, just because it is the only quiet place of the day! I have Bible notes on my phone. I see this quiet time as setting the pace and priorities for the day, remembering that this is all God's.

Martin makes use of his four-mile cycle to work each way. 'I find cycling a good time to think about and pray about specific things – as long as I can switch off and avoid crashing.'

We applaud this versatile and imaginative approach to prayer. At the same time there are dangers in prayer that is limited to prayer 'on the go'. It needs to be supplemented by more concentrated times when we devote our attention to focusing on God alone, without distraction. If arrow prayers become our normative style of prayer, we can easily end up sending God a stream of requests, neglecting to appreciate him for who he is. Adoration, confession and thanksgiving should be the soil from which supplication flows.

Several entrepreneurs do set time apart on a regular daily basis. For some it is first thing in the morning, following the example of Jesus: 'In the morning, while it was still very dark, he got up and went out to a deserted place, and there he prayed' (Mark 1:35). Others find it more congenial to pray in the evening. For them, ending the day in this way feels natural and appropriate: 'Prayer flows quite easily then.' Another makes his main time of prayer for employees in the evenings, walking round the business, going to each person's ramp after they have gone home, and praying for them there.

Every Christian must find a pattern that works for them. Some of us are more 'morning people' than 'evening people', and vice versa. What matters is to find a time of day when we are relatively free of distractions and can give God the whole-hearted and single-minded focus that he deserves.

For most Christians, a quiet time of prayer also includes the element of reading the Bible. Prayer is a two-way communication, where God speaks to us as well as us talking to him. There are ways of disciplining oneself to listen to what God is saying, often in a still small voice (1 Kings 19:12). The main way in which God speaks to us, however, is normally through the words of Scripture, so it is essential to read and feed on the Bible in a sustained and regular way. Our entrepreneurs cited an impressive range of biblical verses and passages which mean a lot to them. One person, Caroline, claimed that 'I wait on God to give me a Scripture for everything that I'm going to do'.

There are other aids to prayer. Two entrepreneurs said they made use of candles. Jeremy has 'a lit candle on my desk, not for decoration, but to remind me to come continually into God's presence. I don't do that as a holy duty, I do that as a necessity.' LingLing often lights a candle as she prays for a particular person – a common practice in the church she attends. She sees it as a sign of hope for that person.

John Carlisle practises meditation three times a day: reflection when he gets up, renewal at lunchtime and review in the evening. He uses the rosary, which he finds 'a great way of meditating'. The rosary beads help to keep in mind all the main events in the story of our salvation. It roots working life in the big picture of God's dealings with humanity.

Jyoti Banerjee believes it is important that we do not narrow ourselves to prayer and Bible study in considering the spiritual disciplines. He is right, and in the remainder of this chapter we shall concentrate on the particular discipline of fasting as well worthy of consideration.

Fasting

Jyoti is one of two entrepreneurs we interviewed who use fasting. He explained:

> We are looking for a new person in one of the organizations I'm involved in. Those of us responsible for the appointment are giving up food for one day on the same day. The idea is that as we fast we pray more about the situation and the appointment.

Their hope is that in looking for the right person, intentionally going without food will help in the process of focusing on God and listening to God.

The other entrepreneur is Gordon. In recent years he has found fasting helpful:

> When there are issues that I want to bring before God, I find just having a conventional quiet time at the beginning of the day not satisfying enough. On the days when I fast I am more

able to talk to God throughout the day. When your stomach groans or you say no to a biscuit, it helps to focus the mind.

Gordon and his wife fasted before a decision to sell a business:

> Prayer and fasting . . . somehow in the spiritual realm led to the potential buyers coming to the fore. We had been thinking of selling the business for some time, but it was when we fasted that the door began to open. We got an approach and eventually negotiated a satisfactory deal.

Fasting is an important supplement to prayer. In the Bible it is usually directed towards seeking God's guidance and help (e.g. 2 Chronicles 20:3–4). It is crucial that it is seen in this way, and not as an aid to dieting; the time spent not eating should be used for praying instead. A day's fasting appears to be particularly helpful when praying about a major decision, appointing key personnel or before the start of a new phase in life, business or otherwise. Moses went without food or drink for forty days when he received God's law on Mount Sinai (Exodus 34:28). Jesus fasted for forty days in the wilderness before he embarked on his ministry. Both were astonishingly long periods of abstinence. The church leaders at Antioch fasted and prayed before the Holy Spirit commanded them to send Paul and Barnabas on their momentous missionary journey (Acts 13:2–3). Likewise, Paul and Barnabas appointed elders in the church that they planted, entrusting them to the Lord with prayer and fasting (Acts 14:23). Fasting is often the prelude to a key divine communication.

In advocating fasting, we need to keep a proper biblical balance. It should not become an empty religious ritual. In Isaiah 58, God deplores fasting that is unaccompanied by righteousness of life:

Is not this the fast that I choose:
> to loose the bonds of injustice,
> to undo the thongs of the yoke,
to let the oppressed go free,
> and to break every yoke?
Is it not to share your bread with the hungry,
> and bring the homeless poor into your house;
when you see the naked, to cover them,
> and not to hide yourself from your own kin?
(Isaiah 58:6–7)

Jesus saw his coming as a reason for festivity, not fasting, because he was the equivalent of a bridegroom (Mark 2:18–19) – a symbol of that being his turning water into wine at the wedding in Cana (John 2:1–11). But he also said: 'The days will come when the bridegroom is taken away,' and, 'they will fast on that day' (Mark 2:20). Yes, he advocated a joyful countenance, not a dismal one: 'when you fast, put oil on your head and wash your face' (Matthew 6:17). But notice that he said 'when you fast', not 'if you fast'. He seems to have expected that his followers would fast from time to time.

At its deepest level, fasting enables the Holy Spirit to reveal to us our true spiritual condition, resulting in brokenness, repentance and a transformed life. King David said: 'I humble myself through fasting' (Psalm 35:13 NIV), and he practised it when in mourning for his adulterous murder of Uriah, and when praying for the survival of the child who was the fruit of his union with Bathsheba (2 Samuel 12:16). Fasting still has a place among believers today. It can add to the spiritual focus and intensity which we bring to important stages of our lives. We encourage entrepreneurs who have never used this valuable discipline to give it a try.

13. I JUST REFUSE TO GIVE UP

In the secular literature on entrepreneurship, certain characteristics common to successful entrepreneurs stand out. John
Hornaday drew up a list of forty-two characteristics in an
influential survey undertaken in 1982. They included, very
prominently, 'self-confident and optimistic', along with
'resourceful and persevering'. More recently, Bolton and
Thompson list entrepreneurs' 'determination in the face of
adversity' among their top ten 'action factors'. They write:

> Entrepreneurs are motivated to succeed; they possess
> determination and self-belief. On the one hand, this is
> a major reason for their success; they refuse to be beaten
> and persevere when 'the going gets tough'. On the other
> hand, this also explains why some would-be entrepreneurs
> fail. They have too much faith in their own ability; they
> believe they are infallible and can do almost anything; they
> refuse to accept they might be wrong; they fail to seek help
> when they need it.

Our research into Christian entrepreneurs reveals similar findings to these larger surveys. When asked, 'What personal characteristics or behaviours do you display that contribute to success in your business life?', nearly half mentioned *perseverance*, or a similar word such as determination, persistence, resilience or tenacity. Perseverance was actually the most cited characteristic, outnumbering other important ones such as innovation and integrity.

Patient endurance

The New Testament has much to say about perseverance. Several of our entrepreneurs were keenly aware of this. The Greek word most often translated as 'perseverance' has the sense of both patient endurance and steadfastness. These three biblical passages illustrate it:

> Therefore, since we have been justified through faith, we have peace with God through our Lord Jesus Christ, through whom we have gained access by faith into this grace in which we now stand. And we boast in the hope of the glory of God. Not only so, but we also glory in our sufferings, because we know that suffering produces perseverance; perseverance, character; and character, hope.
> (Romans 5:1–4 NIV)

> Therefore, since we are surrounded by so great a cloud of witnesses, let us also lay aside every weight and the sin that clings so closely, and let us run with perseverance the race that is set before us, looking to Jesus the pioneer and perfecter of our faith.
> (Hebrews 12:1–2)

> Make every effort to add to your faith goodness; and to
> goodness, knowledge; and to knowledge, self-control; and to
> self-control, perseverance; and to perseverance, godliness; and
> to godliness, mutual affection; and to mutual affection, love.
> (2 Peter 1:5–7 NIV)

A different word for perseverance also occurs, notably in
Paul's list of the fruit of the Spirit in Galatians 5:22. It is most
often translated 'patience' and carries the sense of forbearance
or bearing wrongs patiently.

The context in which the New Testament authors talk
about perseverance is the Christian life in its totality. They
want their readers to persevere as faithful followers of Jesus,
seeking sanctification and not jeopardizing their salvation.
Christian entrepreneurs recognize this, but also see perseverance as relevant to the specific business projects to which they
feel God has called them.

Why is there such a premium on perseverance in business?
Mike Clargo was emphatic that 'Perseverance is purely and
simply discipline. It isn't a nice word. It means more grief,
more hassle, more expenditure of energy; less relaxation, less
indulgence, less luxury. It means giving up things, sacrifice.'

Simon Macaulay said:

> It's really hard being an entrepreneur, because lots of things
> go wrong. You have to make sacrifices with your family. You
> need perseverance, because business is not easy. Things have
> gone wrong lots of times, but on the bad days I just keep
> coming in. Sometimes you just have to persevere when you
> feel frightened, empty, lonely and depressed.

Fortunately, our entrepreneurs seem to have perseverance in
spades. This is what several said about themselves:

- 'I am one of the most bloody-minded people you will ever meet. I just refuse to give up. Every time we come up against a challenge that seems too big or impossible to overcome, God gives me the strength to keep going. He often sends words and pictures through other people to encourage me.'

- 'Tenacity is my hallmark. My wife would agree. She says I'm highly motivated and highly tenacious, and I don't give up easily. There are times when I don't feel I can push on any further, and I honestly feel my heavenly Father with me saying, "We can make this happen."'

- 'I have a "can do" attitude. Determination and doggedness are my key attributes. When I come up against a brick wall, I'm always looking for and finding ways round it.'

- 'I have determination and an almost arrogant belief that we can make a success of the business. For eight years we didn't have much success, but I was determined to keep going. My attitude is: if we have the power and authority of God in our lives, then what *can't* we achieve? My fundamental bottom line is that God is on our side and God wants to change the people that we are involved with.'

On the one hand, entrepreneurs saw perseverance as a quality that was part of their personality; on the other hand, they recognized their need for God's help in their strivings. It is when we try to do things through our own strength that we often fail, whereas 'I can do all things through him who strengthens me' (Philippians 4:13).

Hugh Davidson is a Manxman. He used to run a marketing strategy consultancy, and now runs a charitable trust with his wife Sandra. They work alongside charities such as Oxfam and Save the Children to help women and girls in East India and Bangladesh. Hugh sees *resilience* as one of his key characteristics. Overcoming considerable obstacles, he has seen a joint venture with Oxfam help to triple the income of 4,000 very poor fisherwomen over a six-year period. Interestingly, Hugh sees resilience as a regional characteristic. The Isle of Man is famous for the resilience of its people and Hugh believes he reflects this.

We shall now explore entrepreneurs' perseverance in the face of many different business setbacks: delays, cheating, recession and bankruptcy.

Delays

Martin Clark is Deputy Chief Executive of Allia, a charity that supports social ventures, providing business support, workspace and financial solutions to help social enterprises start, grow and flourish. The charity runs Future Business Centres where this support is concentrated in Cambridge and Peterborough. Establishing the Cambridge centre proved really difficult. Martin tells the story:

> This building has been eleven years in the planning. We bought a site in town which we thought was the right place. It took three years to move from vision to actually having a place where we could build the new centre. There were all kinds of problems in planning. The residents opposed it. We got permission and then had it taken away from us. We could and should have given up, really, but we were very, very determined to persevere. And finally we found another site. In between we found ways to use empty buildings to provide low-cost space, to prove the need. We would like to have delivered the permanent business space for social enterprises

much earlier, so we had eleven years of not succeeding before it worked. At the launch the chief executive said I'd held the vision all that time.

Even when the turf-cutting launch event occurred with the mayor putting his spade in the ground, Allia continued to be beset by delays:

> The next day the building company told us that they didn't think we had enough money and they weren't confident we could pay for the project, so they didn't start. In fact they didn't start for another nine months! To have an event where you went public with something and then were seen to backtrack was awful. But we persevered.

Cheating

Another test of resilience is the experience of being cheated. Five of the fifty entrepreneurs mentioned this among their worst experiences in business. They had been let down by people they considered friends or partners. In three of the five cases, large sums of money were involved: entrepreneurs considered they had been swindled out of thousands of pounds which had never been repaid. Sadly, two of the individuals identified as cheats were professing Christians.

In another case, the sums were smaller, but a subcontractor felt he had been exploited by an older, more experienced contractor who had once been his mentor. In the final case, two employees who left Phil's company broke their word by setting up a competing company and poaching other staff.

'Even my bosom friend in whom I trusted, who ate of my bread, has lifted the heel against me' (Psalm 41:9). These are words that the New Testament applies to Jesus' relationship with Judas (John 13:18). The experience of being betrayed by a friend is profoundly painful, but the entrepreneurs who talked about this had all found the strength to carry on. Two of them also spoke of discovering the grace to forgive those who had wronged them.

Recession

For most of the entrepreneurs who were running companies during the global financial crisis, the years 2006–8 were very difficult. Most experienced substantial reduction in customer demand and subsequent cash-flow problems. Gary Grant's The Entertainer nearly went the way of other toy retailers – down the plughole. Gary says:

> Business dived. It wasn't of our doing. There was a lack of confidence in society, in the country, in the world generally. Banks were going bust, insurance companies were going bust. That was a very stressful time and we never budgeted while we cut back. We just had to go into survival mode.

Inevitably the company had to make some staff redundant. It was during that period that Gary sent an email to staff from head office: ' "I don't know whether you pray but we are going to get together at lunchtime for a prayer meeting." Expecting there to be me, my wife and two sons, I put a few chairs out and thirty staff turned up.' That seems to have been the turning point.

Val King's Rooflight company found 2008–9 very hard. Val says that 'people were literally not buying construction materials at all'. She believes very tight management controls saved the company.

We took away a lot of the perks for staff: free fruit, physio and obviously bonuses. It was like taking away all the privileges. The reaction wasn't that negative, because people understood that everyone was suffering and they felt lucky that they still had a job.

It was a very hard time, 'absolutely hard', but Val and Rooflight pulled through.

In 2006, Barry made an acquisition that doubled the size of his car group. They borrowed heavily to carry out the expansion, so were highly leveraged. Barry says:

Then the crisis comes, and you go wow, we are in trouble. We had to make people redundant. The suffering could have been more evenly shared if the company had gone into administration; instead we made the tough call to make sixty-three people redundant. Looking into people's eyes and saying sorry is the toughest part of business. Behind each face is a real person with real kids and real rent to pay.

In retrospect, Barry is more philosophical:

You have to persevere through the bad times. In retail you will have good times when the economy is good and bad times when the economy is bad. You need to show character and perseverance to get through the difficult season and reach the next season of plenty.

Bankruptcy

Christian faith is no guarantee of corporate survival. Several entrepreneurs had experienced the worst that business life can throw at you, with their company going bankrupt. For Simon

Lawson it happened in 1993, even though the company was trading profitably. Bankruptcy was the effect of an investment in commercial property that failed due to the sudden rise in UK interest rates. Lawsons also suffered from the actions of a 'dodgy accountant'. However, a restarted company rose like a phoenix from the ashes of the old. Simon's father John was 'conscience stricken' by the effect of the collapse on his creditors. He invited all the creditors to invoice the new company for their outstanding debts, and honoured these as soon as Lawsons could afford it – a true act of integrity. In retrospect Simon sees the company going bust as a time of *cleansing*: ultimately he and the company emerged stronger because of it.

Gordon has experienced not one but two major liquidations that 'brought us to our knees'. He is refreshingly honest, admitting that he was at fault on both occasions. In the early 1990s his garment-processing business appeared to be doing extremely well – 'on the peak of a wave' – but it was then hit by the economic downturn and the rise in interest rates. The business had debts of £1.5 million, but Gordon worked with the liquidator and managed to find someone to restart the company, 55% of the debts being written off. The focus of the new company was warehousing, diversifying successfully through the late 1990s and 2000s. Eventually, however, Gordon bought two transport companies that did not turn out to be sound investments; one was located in a building that required major repairs, and the other had a workforce that followed many restrictive practices. Gordon employed some highly paid professionals who could not retrieve the situation. What saved him second time round was that the local council offered to buy a mill that he owned and the purchase went through quickly. Gordon says: 'The money we got in came within a stone's throw of wiping out the indebtedness I had incurred on the transport companies.' He is grateful to God for – as he sees it – saving him from the consequences of his overconfidence.

Andrew Tanswell has also experienced corporate failure. This was with ToughStuff, and was extremely frustrating because the company seemed to be doing very well. Richard featured it in *Faith, Hope and the Global Economy* as an excellent example of a company producing high-quality durable products using solar energy, meeting a real need in rural Africa. Andrew says:

> We were growing quite rapidly across Africa and were working in ten countries, but then in the space of a few months we incurred massive bad debts across three countries, because in those countries interest rates were either doubling or trebling. We ran out of cash and had to go into liquidation.

Notice a common theme among companies that hit trouble: the damage that a hike in interest rates can cause. The situation was distressing for Andrew. 'Even when it was done and dusted, we still grieved over it, partly because it takes a while to close a company down.' It led to a process of heart-searching, seeking to learn lessons from mistakes; but Andrew still felt called to continue in the same field. He is now Chief Executive of PoaPower, which operates on a pay-as-you-go basis and provides abundant, clean and affordable energy to off-grid, low-income consumers in the Global South. Essentially it is a refinement of what Andrew did before, and has secured a hefty investment from the Global Investment Fund.

Andrew's reflection is that 'in the very hard times God has always kept me when I feel I'm falling'. Aware that he has had a mixture of successes and failures, he seeks to follow the advice contained in Rudyard Kipling's poem 'If', to treat the two imposters of triumph and disaster just the same. He perseveres, keeping the goal of bringing economic and ecological transformation to sub-Saharan Africa uppermost in his mind.

A persistent God

For Richard Leftley, the quality of persistence or perseverance is exemplified in God's own character. He points out: 'God never gives up on us. I mean, we're all sinners, we're all fallen and we continue to disappoint him, but he's always there waiting for our return.' He cites the parable of the prodigal son who squanders his father's inheritance, but the father sees his son a long way off and runs to welcome him back. Richard also mentions Jonah, who did not want to do what God told him, but God 'pursued him; he kept going after Jonah until he was obedient'. Richard finds being an entrepreneur exhausting, certainly his own area of micro-insurance: 'Doing something which no-one's done before in a field where everyone has said it won't work, but refusing to listen to that, reflecting on what you think is the truth, asking friends and praying with them; then being persistent.'

Admirable though the quality of perseverance may be, it begs the question of how long we should persist with commercial ideas that are just not working. Richard shrewdly observes that 'it's fine to fail, but it's a really massive mistake to fail slowly – because failing slowly will kill you, it will use all your money and all your resources'. So sometimes God-given perseverance may take the form of being absolutely true to a goal, the vision of what one wants to achieve, while being extremely flexible about the details of how it is achieved. It means having a Plan B when Plan A does not work.

Hopefulness

It is possible to think about perseverance in a rather negative way, as being all about gritting your teeth, showing a stiff upper lip and putting up with enormous difficulties. But that is not how most of the entrepreneurs we interviewed talked about perseverance.

Earlier we quoted Simon Macaulay, who admitted that it is really hard being an entrepreneur, because many things go wrong. However, he also said: 'Entrepreneurs are optimistic. I am optimistic. You have to be optimistic. You have to be good at selling, because you must have the confidence to go and knock on the door.' In the midst of difficulties, Simon says he loves coming into work.

When asked which characteristics contributed to her success in business, Val put 'having a positive mental attitude' at the top of her list. 'If you are a business leader and don't feel a positive attitude then you can't really lead people. People don't want to follow someone who is negative.' Val says it helps that she really enjoys working with people. In the midst of the difficult situation she experienced in the 2008 recession, when Rooflight had to make some staff redundant, she was encouraged by hearing a business leaders' talk that stressed the importance of a positive attitude. This gave her 'a kick up the backside' which helped her to lead Rooflight well in a time of crisis. She also emphasizes the importance of perspective when making difficult choices. She sometimes says 'No-one's going to die if we make a wrong decision' to prevent colleagues being paralysed into *indecision.*

Sir Peter Vardy is a successful motor group CEO. Based in Sunderland, he took over a garage from his father Reg Vardy in 1976 and built a national group of 100 dealerships employing 6,000 people before selling out in 2006. He established four academies in the north of England and is currently investing in a new charity, Safe Families for Children. Sir Peter is another entrepreneur who emphasizes perseverance. He says:

> You need a vision, then a strategy. Vision without strategy is just hallucination. But then you need the drive and determination to deliver. You have to inspire your team and make sure they believe in your vision. A leader is not a leader if no-one is following. He has merely gone for a walk. Your goals have to be achievable. We took over car dealerships selling forty cars a month and took sales up to 200 per month. We all bought in to BHAGs (Big Hairy Audacious Goals) which made for an exciting ride!

The entrepreneur we know with the most positive mindset, however, is almost certainly Mark Mitchell. The standard test of whether someone has an optimistic or pessimistic outlook is usually deemed to be the glass that contains 50% of water. The pessimist sees it as half empty while the optimist sees it as half full. Entrepreneurs are almost invariably 'half full' people. For Mark, 'the glass isn't just half full, it's overflowing'. He says:

> I like the excitement of business life, and that's why I'm drawn to it. I see a Christian entrepreneur as waking up in the morning and – perhaps arrogantly or naively – thinking it's going to be a great day. I'm going to meet with success today. And when faith is overlaid with that, you understand that you need to do things with integrity, credibility and a biblical warmth; you need to be doing business God's way.

'I know the plans I have for you'

Perseverance and hope are closely connected. It is interesting that they occur together in Romans 5:1–4. The word that links them is 'character': 'suffering produces perseverance; perseverance, character; and character, hope'. People who persevere do so because they are hopeful of an ultimately positive outcome, and the character they develop enables them to keep hoping even when the outlook is bleak. In the overall context of the Christian life, hope is not a delusion, because we have already tasted the Lord's goodness. As Paul goes on to say in Romans 5:5: 'hope does not disappoint us, because God's love has been poured into our hearts through the Holy Spirit that has been given to us.'

For our Christian entrepreneurs, the biblical passage communicating hope which was cited most often was Jeremiah 29:11: 'For surely I know the plans I have for you, says the LORD, plans for your welfare and not for harm, to give you a future with hope.' One entrepreneur said he had this verse written through the business, on the pen that he used every day. 'It's the verse that was there when we founded the business, and the verse that's kept us going through the hard times.'

In its original context, the verse was directed to Jewish exiles in Babylon, in the sixth century BC. It served to sustain God's people who had gone astray, who were down on their luck and down on their knees. Jeremiah tells them that they will have to serve a seventy-year period of exile, after which they will be able to return to Jerusalem. In the meantime, he exhorts the exiles to get stuck into life in Babylon: 'Build houses and live in them; plant gardens and eat what they produce. Take wives and have sons and daughters' (Jeremiah 29:5–6). He exhorts them to 'seek the welfare of the city where I have sent you into exile, and pray to the LORD on its behalf, for in its welfare you will find your welfare' (Jeremiah 29:7).

Note that this is a collective or group context. Today Christians often apply Jeremiah 29:11 to themselves in an individualist way, but a collective application is more appropriate. It serves as an excellent brief for Christians who are immersed in business. Such a working life may sometimes feel like exile, and they may feel that they are strangers in an alien land, but they should seek the welfare of the place where they work; in doing that they will discover their own welfare. Entrepreneurs can immerse themselves fully in the challenges of the present, secure in the confidence that God has their future in his hands. This is a great reason for hope.

14. SO YOU'VE GOT AN ENTREPRENEUR IN YOUR CHURCH?

We have written this book mainly for entrepreneurs and would-be entrepreneurs. You are our primary audience. In this chapter, however, we shall target our remarks in the direction of church leaders who have actual entrepreneurs and aspiring entrepreneurs in their congregations. So we encourage our entrepreneur readers to show their church leaders this chapter. If that leads them to read the whole book, excellent! A warning, though: this chapter may make uncomfortable reading.

Kina asked our entrepreneurs the question: 'How do you view the attitude of the church towards you? Negative or positive?' Answers to this question diverged sharply. Responses divided into three groups.

A positive experience

For ten of the entrepreneurs the answer was definitely positive. 'Extremely positive and supportive,' said one. Interestingly, a disproportionate number of the ten were women. 'Fine,' said LingLing. 'I love my local church and they love me' – a comment which reflects her friendly, sunny disposition. Natasha's experience of her church is that it is 'so encouraging'. Rebeca's reply was 'Pretty good. My priest recently attended a promotion event I ran and handed out flowers!' Caroline was equally positive: 'The church is now realizing increasingly that they need entrepreneurs and they need business.'

Because the sample of women in our survey was quite small, we hesitate to read too much into this. But it may be that church leaders are more likely to encourage female entrepreneurs because they see them as a minority group in need of support. Perhaps they see men as more able to stand on their own two feet, and less in need of affirmation.

Women also tended to interpret the question more along the lines of the support they received from their local church. The male entrepreneurs we interviewed certainly had that in mind, but tended to have the wider, institutional church in view as well.

Mixed – but slowly improving

The second group, numbering about fifteen entrepreneurs, represented a mixed picture. Some said: 'Neutral – neither positive nor negative.' One thought long and hard and then said: 'Kind of neutral, becoming slightly more positive.' Several entrepreneurs had had negative experiences in the past, but felt the church was slowly improving. One said: 'It helps that our current church leader is an entrepreneur and that Archbishop Justin Welby "gets" business. Our previous vicar didn't understand.'

Welby's informed and sympathetic understanding of business was mentioned by two other interviewees as contributing to a gradual change of attitude. Credit was also given to various 'faith and work' organizations, including Faith in Business. The London Institute for Contemporary Christianity was the most frequently cited. David Bishop said the situation in his local church had improved markedly after they did Mark Greene's God at Work course, followed by Fruitfulness on the Frontline. The church changed its mission statement to 'empowering, equipping and enabling people for whole life discipleship'.

Peter's response was interesting, especially coming from one so young: 'Both negative and positive. Some members of the congregation are massively supportive of what I do – they have provided me with plenty of custom. But I've never been affirmed that what I do contributes to the kingdom of God.' Peter has been looking in vain for church leaders to set the work he does in an overall theological perspective.

Disappointment

Sadly, the majority message – reflected in the replies of half our sample – was that the church's attitude to them as entrepreneurs was negative.

One entrepreneur was quite outspoken. His response is striking because he attends a large evangelical church with a fine reputation:

> I'm hugely disappointed about the way the church treats
> business and talks about entrepreneurs or people in business.
> I think it's really detrimental, and it annoys me. For instance,
> the people the church pulls out to pray for on a Sunday
> morning are those going off for ten years to set up a mission
> hospital or something similar. Highlighting such people sends
> an unfortunate message to others. I think the church is blind

to the impact that Christian business owners can have: it should see equipping, empowering, instructing and enabling business leaders as a priority. If you want to get people out of poverty then you need employment. You need to enable people to work their way out of poverty. I had a very upsetting experience recently when a man told me he'd been in business for forty-five years as a managing director and every day he'd been made to feel like a second-class citizen compared to a pastor or missionary. I don't want anyone else to live like that because I can see how God uses business for expanding his kingdom.

These are strong words, repeated in different ways by several other entrepreneurs. One said:

Entrepreneurs are ignored. Lots of attention is given to teaching, healthcare, what you might describe as vocational careers. It feels like people don't know how to talk about business in a positive way. They are nervous of how things like money can become idolatrous. You don't hear stories about the positive aspects of business. One challenge I feel is in church home groups. Most people who come are employees, and they often share about their difficulties at work. This doesn't leave a lot of room for business owners and managers who are losing sleep as well. They are often struggling to make tough decisions and trying to do what is right.

Another entrepreneur said he felt the church was not so much negative or hostile as indifferent, which is actually worse.

If the church was openly antagonistic, you could debate and argue about that. Instead it's cloistered in its own outlook and environment, where it doesn't bother to have a view about business. Yet business plays an enormous part in people's lives. Business is one way of reaching people, so the Church can't afford to ignore business if it wants to impact people's lives.

The reasons why

Why have our entrepreneurs encountered so much negativity in the church? Their answers to Kina's follow-up question, 'Do you think the church has mishandled the topic of money and business?', shed light on this.

A persistent theme was that the church lacks a fundamental appreciation of what business does. So we heard:

- 'People need to realize that business creates jobs and has a positive impact on social betterment for everybody. It helps create wealth for spending on public services. If your talent is running a good company and creating a new product, that is a positive thing for the benefit of all.'
- 'The church needs to appreciate that money has to come from somewhere. Wealth has to be created.'
- 'Often the church doesn't seem to understand the necessity of profit. Profit is a measure of efficiency. It's not wrong, it's not evil, it's not exploiting people. It's a sign that you're operating better than other people. There's nothing wrong with profit; the key thing is to use profits wisely.'

Over the many years that Ridley Hall has been running Faith in Business, Richard has repeatedly come across these attitudes in church circles. The attitude to business varies from outright hostility to cautious suspicion to plain indifference. Taken overall, there is a failure to appreciate properly the role of profit in running a successful company and the role of wealth creation in resourcing a healthy nation. While some church leaders protest that they *do* understand these things, it might be helpful if they affirmed them more often. What goes unsaid is often assumed not to be understood.

The other message to come through loud and clear was that entrepreneurs often feel appreciated only for the financial support they are potentially able to provide. Note these responses:

- 'The church doesn't seem to have anything to say about money other than asking for it.'
- 'Sometimes they view us a bit like an open cheque book. They come to us when they want a project financed.'
- 'Many ministers see business as a funding source for mission, rather than as a mission-field itself.'

This is sad. Entrepreneurs often *are* willing to give generously to worthy causes – but if church leaders only appreciate the work they do because of the funding they are able to offer, entrepreneurs are being viewed as a means to an end. The church is failing to appreciate entrepreneurial activity for its intrinsic value and for the common good. This is hurtful.

Encourage one another

The Bible has much to say when it comes to instructing mutual encouragement. 'Therefore encourage one another and build up each other, as indeed you are doing' (1 Thessalonians 5:11). All Christians need encouraging. This can be done in a general way, but it has greater impact when encouragement takes a specific form – either through a personal word to individuals, or a message specially tailored to a particular group. Church leaders need to include entrepreneurs – along with other individuals and very different groups – amidst their radius of encouragement. In return, entrepreneurs should show similar concern for their church leaders. Paul continues to the Thessalonians: 'We appeal to you, brothers and sisters, to respect those who labour among you, and have charge of you in the Lord and admonish you; esteem them very highly in love because of their work' (1 Thessalonians 5:12–13). Entrepreneurs and church leaders are both carrying the burdens and joys of leadership, each in their distinctive spheres. They should have much to offer each other.

The book of Hebrews is strong on the theme of encouragement.

> But exhort one another every day . . . so that none of you
> may be hardened by the deceitfulness of sin.
> (Hebrews 3:13)

> Let us hold fast to the confession of our hope without
> wavering, for he who has promised is faithful. And let
> us consider how to provoke one another to love and good
> deeds, not neglecting to meet together, as is the habit of
> some, but encouraging one another, and all the more as
> you see the Day approaching.
> (Hebrews 10:23–25)

Encouragement is not just about saying positive things to one another, though that may often be an appropriate starting point. It will also include elements of warning, rebuke, pointing out where one's brother or sister may be in danger of falling into sin. Paradoxically, entrepreneurs will often be encouraged if their church leaders care enough or are perceptive enough to show them when they are deceiving themselves.

Entrepreneurs are resourceful people, and where neglected will often find ways of coping, sometimes by forming their own support networks – surrounding themselves with people who do understand. However, the fact that half our sample had such negative experiences of the church is not a healthy situation. The church is a body where everybody's contribution should be appreciated and affirmed. As 1 Corinthians 12 teaches, it is a body with many different members. The church roles that Paul lists – apostles, prophets, teachers, etc. – have their business counterparts. All have crucial parts to play to the glory of God.

Doing better

So how can church leaders do better? Plenty of answers were forthcoming.

The first answer that entrepreneurs gave was to *listen*. Make time to spend with entrepreneurs and talk with them. That is the way to understand better what their work is and what makes them tick. Ideally, spend time with them in their place of work. Invite yourself to work-shadow entrepreneurs for a day or half-day, and we are sure they will be only too delighted to oblige. Equally worthwhile is to have lunch with them during a weekday, at a pub or restaurant near their workplace. The proximity to work helps people speak frankly about the pressures and challenges they face; open disclosure comes less easily in a church context.

The second suggestion is to *give entrepreneurs a voice in the church*. This could consist of a series of meetings where they tell their stories, discuss their problems and enthuse about their opportunities. They could be included in interviews during a Sunday morning service. David Bishop described two initiatives that have taken place in his church. One is

TTT – This Time Tomorrow. Each Sunday, a member of the congregation explains what they will be doing at 11 am on a Monday morning. It is a great way for church members to gain insight into the work that others do. A variation is TTS – Time To Share. Christians share either a good news story or a bad news story – a workplace incident that has happened to them during the past week.

The third proposal follows from the second, and that is to *pray*. Explaining what they do at work or what has gone wrong at work leads church members to request prayer for their situation. Why not enlist the people of God to marshal the forces of prayer in resisting evil and advancing the kingdom? One entrepreneur expressed real gratitude for 'the prayer warriors in our church, retired folk who thankfully make time for these things'. Church leaders should encourage this. A support group may make time to pray with individual entrepreneurs – along with other people – on a one-to-one basis. Offering to pray can even be done with business owners who never darken the doors of a church. Richard knows one Anglican vicar who wrote to every company on the business park in his parish, asking what they would like the church to pray for. He received appreciative and constructive replies from many businesspeople who were not in fact believers, but were pleased that the church was showing an interest in what they were doing.

The fourth idea is to *make biblical teaching more relevant*. This is a challenge for many church leaders because their training has not included much in the area of business. Hopefully graduates of Ridley Hall have enjoyed a different experience! Our website, <www.faith-in-business.org>, contains a wealth of useful material, including short reflections on biblical passages which have a clear but often unexplored application to business. One preaching tip is to have a range of occupational situations in view when applying any particular message. Envisage what this applied truth might mean for people in, say, three different types of job.

Paul provides an example of this in 2 Timothy 2:1–7. He shows what the virtue of perseverance means in three different contexts: military, sporting and agricultural. He illustrates his central message of being strong in the grace of the Lord Jesus with reference to a soldier ('No one serving in the army gets entangled in everyday affairs'), an athlete ('No one is crowned without competing according to the rules') and a farmer ('It is the farmer who does the work who ought to have the first share of the crops'). Imaginative application is a key part of preaching.

The fifth suggestion is to *be open to the fact that God might seriously be calling people beyond the confines of the church*. One entrepreneur said bluntly:

> Instead of encouraging the brightest and best to become worship leaders, why don't they encourage them to become business leaders? For me, coming to work is equally as important as turning up to church on Sunday, and the things I do in this office are my worship.

We agree, and the church may need to take something of a back seat in making that point. It is interesting that when Paul uses the word 'worship' in Romans 12:1–2 ('present your bodies as a living sacrifice, holy and acceptable to God, which is your spiritual worship'), he is not talking about a Sunday act of worship, but about Christians' dedication of their whole lives every day.

Finally, church leaders should *recognize that entrepreneurs may have a significant role to play in church leadership*. This will not usually be in terms of official roles, but entrepreneurs may have a contribution to make in helping to shape a local church's direction and vision. They will often think 'outside the box', they will be clear on the need for high standards, and they know how to investigate and identify resources. Many church leaders shy away from involving entrepreneurs because they are strong characters, even – on their own admission – mavericks. But where God guides, it is worth taking the risk. Entrepreneurs may have crucial insights regarding the church's mission. This leads us to the theme of our final chapter.

15. BECOMING THE BEST YOU CAN BE

God is raising up a new workforce of men and women from around the world. These men and women are on a mission for God's glory in and through business. Christian leaders in business, church, missions and beyond have all concurred that God is at work and business as mission is dynamically meeting the various needs of a world in desperate need of the whole Gospel!

All countries and cultures have entrepreneurial people. These people (or potential ones) hold some of the most critical keys to potentially demonstrate the kingdom of God.

These two quotations come from Lausanne Occasional Paper no. 59, *Business as Mission*. The Lausanne Movement is an international movement committed to energizing the whole church to take the whole gospel to the whole world. It grew out of a congress held in Lausanne, Switzerland, in 1974; this produced the Lausanne Covenant. Since then it has held several further meetings and developed several distinctive strands, including a business strand. Business as Mission is now a global movement in its own right.

So far in this book we have made sparing use of the word 'mission', but the inexorable logic of our research project is that business does indeed have a major role to play in God's mission. Entrepreneurs are, or should be, at the forefront of this.

We fully understand that some of you who are entrepreneurs may read this with a sinking feeling in your heart. Starting and running a business is a very demanding task. Surely you have enough to worry about without being saddled with a major responsibility for mission? Are we placing upon you a burden that is simply too much to bear? Of course, we recognize that much of the time in running a business you are involved with matters of fine detail which demand your careful attention: financial, technical and personnel issues that may appear far removed from a theology of mission. So let us clear up some possible misunderstandings.

Two misunderstandings

The first misunderstanding concerns *the nature of mission*. Mission used to be understood as a synonym for evangelism. We certainly believe that it includes evangelism, sharing the gospel of Jesus Christ by personal witness, with the hope that others may become Christians. But the term 'mission' is now used more widely, to mean God's plan and purpose to transform the whole of his creation. It does not just denote the changing of individuals; it is about transforming communities, cultures and countries so that God's will is done on earth, as well as in heaven. The Business as Mission movement has a holistic understanding of mission; it is not just about using business as a tool for evangelism. The business itself matters. The business must provide a useful product or service and bring glory to God; otherwise the personal witness of Christians who work for the business will carry no credibility.

The second misunderstanding concerns *the nature of being a Christian*. Christianity has often been considered a private matter, with individuals being free to opt into as much or as little Christian commitment as they like. Becoming a follower of Jesus Christ is not like that. In choosing to follow Jesus, we are integrated into a much bigger picture. We become part of the worldwide body of the people of God, charged with rescuing God's world from the sorry mess into which it has fallen. As individuals, we may only be able to play a small part in restoring God's world, but let's not abdicate our responsibility or underestimate what we can do. In *Faith, Hope and the Global Economy*, Richard has shown how every episode in the biblical story of salvation has something important, challenging and hopeful to say about business. We are active players in this biblical drama, able to affect society for good by stimulating enterprise, reducing poverty, promoting integrity and ensuring sustainability, as well as making disciples.

Three commands

God's mission is often summed up in the key biblical commands that are called the Creation Mandate, the Great Commandment and the Great Commission.

The Creation Mandate – sometimes called the Cultural Mandate – is Genesis 1:28: 'Be fruitful and multiply, and fill the earth and subdue it; and have dominion over the fish of the sea and over the birds of the air and over every living thing that moves upon the earth.' To this may be added

Genesis 2:15, where 'The LORD God took the man and put him in the garden of Eden to till it and keep it'. From these two verses flows the idea of human beings exercising steward-ship over creation. They subdue the earth; they till and keep the garden. This mandate is carried out in many different ways by all sorts of people, but in the course of world history, business is the primary vehicle through which the earth's resources have been developed. In extracting and refining the material resources God has embedded within his world, humanity's commercial instincts have come to the fore. People have developed these resources into products that enhance the quality of life, from the wearing of precious jewels to the provision of electricity. They have made money out of this. So business has assumed a major responsibility for exercising the creation mandate. It has a mixed record on this score. Often it has fulfilled the mandate selfishly and carelessly. But human beings do also have the ability to deliver the creation mandate responsibly, creatively and for the good of all.

The Great Commandment is found in Mark 12:28–34. This is Jesus' response to a lawyer's question: 'Which command-ment is the first of all?'

> Jesus answered, 'The first is, "Hear, O Israel: the Lord our
> God, the Lord is one; you shall love the Lord your God with
> all your heart, and with all your soul, and with all your mind,
> and with all your strength." The second is this, "You shall love
> your neighbour as yourself." There is no other commandment
> greater than these.'

In citing the first commandment, to love God, Jesus was following common Jewish practice; the Jews of his day regularly recited Deuteronomy 6:4, which was known as the Shema. In giving special prominence to loving your neighbour,

Jesus was being more innovative. Here he takes a commandment that was hidden away in the book of Leviticus (19:18–19), between some very specific injunctions about not taking vengeance and not letting animals breed with a different kind, and sets up love of neighbour as absolutely central. He saw love of God and love of neighbour as belonging together; the latter follows from the former. In the parable he told in reply to the lawyer's follow-up question, the story of the good Samaritan (Luke 10:29–37), he made clear that 'neighbour' did not simply mean the fellow Israelite who lived next door. It included the person you were inclined to think of as your enemy. This has important implications for business. We have shown earlier how love of neighbour extends to all the stakeholder relationships in business. Indeed, precisely because a company has contact with such a wide range of people, it provides enormous opportunity for loving your neighbour.

The Great Commission consists of Jesus' final words to his disciples:

> Jesus came and said to them, 'All authority in heaven and on
> earth has been given to me. Go therefore and make disciples
> of all nations, baptizing them in the name of the Father
> and of the Son and of the Holy Spirit, and teaching them to
> obey everything that I have commanded you. And remember,
> I am with you always, to the end of the age.'
> (Matthew 28:18–20)

Christians down the ages have seen this as a command not just for Jesus' original disciples but for all his subsequent followers. Note how Jesus does not say, 'Go and make converts of all nations', even though conversion is an important stage in the process. He tells his disciples to *make disciples* – in other words, faithful and intimate followers. The disciples are both to baptize and to teach others to obey everything that Jesus had commanded them. In short, quality of Christian life matters. Sadly, over the centuries, all too many converts who are Christians in name have let Jesus down by what they have done. Christians who work in business have a responsibility to be obedient followers, just like Christians in every other walk of life. Entrepreneurs have a special responsibility because they set an example.

Lawyer Matthew Turnour takes very seriously the responsibility to disciple people in the workplace. He says every business has a way of doing things and a culture into which employees are discipled. 'If a person comes from a particular firm or works for a particular partner it is frequently possible to accurately predict how they are likely to behave in a particular context.' They have been trained and mentored (what Christians call 'discipled') into the ways of that firm or partner.

> The question is not whether discipling takes place, but rather, 'What are employees like after they have been discipled?' School leavers and graduates come to us at eighteen or twenty-three years of age. They stay with us for a period and as their first boss we shape their attitudes to work, clients, the profession, service, colleagues, money and many other things.

That is discipleship in the workplace, so 'Christians should be very intentional not just about their formal mentoring and their training but about the example they set in all that they do'.

This highlights the responsibility entrepreneurs have towards junior staff, in nurturing them and teaching them godly values. The discipling process may be more clear cut in the case of professional service firms than other companies, but something like this occurs in most types of business. What sort of disciples are you producing?

Four kingdom imperatives

As well as these three commands, we would like to remind you of the four ways of advancing the kingdom mentioned in chapter 6. These emerged from the fifty interviews. Entrepreneurs believed they were advancing the kingdom of God by:

1. making the world a better place – through providing an excellent product or service;
2. embodying Christian values – expressed in the highest standards of business ethics which flow from Christian faith;
3. witnessing by word – taking opportunities to speak about the Christian faith as and when appropriate;
4. charitable giving – using a generous proportion of profits to support worthy charitable causes, including Christian ones.

All these are important aspects of advancing the kingdom in this world. We applaud what Christian entrepreneurs are doing in each area. We have also suggested that there may be scope for some entrepreneurs to embrace more of these objectives. In a holistic understanding of mission, there is a place not just for one or two of these, but for all four. Can you expand your mission statement, whether public or private, to include them all? We urge you to consider this seriously.

Mission – a strategic role for entrepreneurs

Entrepreneurs are influential men and women. The nature of their role is that they touch many people's lives. They are often outgoing, confident people who are good at talking to others and making things happen. In view of this, it is surprising that entrepreneurs do not feature more in the church's strategy for mission.

In the last chapter we called on church leaders to do more to affirm and encourage entrepreneurs in their congregations. Now we wish to go a stage further. We suggest they seek ways to include entrepreneurs in their thinking about mission and planning of mission initiatives. The church needs people who are prepared to think 'outside the box', to be courageous and innovative. Entrepreneurs have a proven record in this respect.

In particular, we urge church leaders who are advancing new thinking in mission – as in the fresh expressions or pioneer ministry movements – to take entrepreneurs on board in their thinking. Sadly, most mainstream theologies of mission accord little place for business. The mission theologian who comes closest, perhaps, is Christopher Wright, in his *Biblical Theology for Life: The Mission of God's People*. This includes a helpful chapter on 'People who Live and Work in the Public Square', where he says to Christians in the everyday working world:

> Your daily work matters because it matters to God. It has its own intrinsic value and worth. If it contributes in any way to the needs of society, the service of others, the stewardship of the earth's resources, then it has some place in God's plans for this creation and in the new creation. And if you do it conscientiously as a disciple of Jesus, bearing witness to him, being always ready to give an answer to those who enquire about your faith, and being willing to suffer for Christ if called to – then he will enable your life to bear fruit in ways you may never be aware of. You are engaged in the mission of God's people.

We fully agree. But we also feel that the role of Christian businesspeople in general and entrepreneurs in particular deserves special mention.

This lack of joined-up thinking is the more surprising because Business as Mission has been around since the turn of the century, and coexists with much of the latest missionary thinking in the Lausanne movement. However, we do not wish to end on a negative or pessimistic note about this. There is clearly scope for plenty of fruitful dialogue among mission-minded Christians, across the business and academic communities. In the meantime we encourage Christian entrepreneurs not to be downcast. If you feel you have an important contribution or insight to make to your church's thinking and practice about mission, do not be inhibited – keep speaking out.

Becoming the best you can be

One of our interviewees, David Henderson, runs a personal development consultancy called Becoming the Best You Can Be. A great title and a wonderful aspiration! That is our parting wish for all the readers of this book, both actual entrepreneurs and aspiring entrepreneurs.

God has given you special gifts and talents to use in his service. He has given you ideas for how you can make the world a better place. He has put you into contact with many people on whom you can have a positive Christian influence. Become the Best You Can Be. In God's good purpose, that could well exceed your wildest imagination.

> Now to him who by the power at work within us is able
> to accomplish abundantly far more than all that we ask or
> imagine, to him be glory in the church and in Christ Jesus
> to all generations, forever and ever. Amen.
> (Ephesians 3:20–21)

BIBLIOGRAPHY

Books

Robert Banks, *God the Worker: Journeys into the Heart, Mind and Imagination of God*, Judson Press, 1994.

Bill Bolton and John Thompson, *Entrepreneurs: Talent, Temperament, Technique*, 2nd ed., Elsevier Butterworth-Heinemann, 2004.

Ian Bradley, *Enlightened Entrepreneurs: Business Ethics in Victorian Britain*, 2nd ed., Lion, 2007.

Richard Branson, *Business Stripped Bare: Adventures of a Global Entrepreneur*, Virgin Books, 2009.

Deborah Cadbury, *Chocolate Wars: From Cadbury to Kraft – 200 Years of Swift Success and Bitter Rivalry*, HarperPress, 2011.

John Carlisle and Robert Parker, *Beyond Negotiation: Redeeming Customer–Supplier Relationships*, John Wiley & Sons, 1989.

Martin Clark, *The Social Entrepreneur Revolution: Doing Good by Making Money, Making Money by Doing Good*, Marshall Cavendish, 2009.

Shane Clifton, 'Pentecostal Approaches to Economics', *The Oxford Handbook of Christianity and Economics* (ed. Paul Oslington), Oxford University Press, 2014, ch. 15.

Roy Coad, *Laing: The Biography of Sir John W. Laing, CBE (1879–1978)*, Hodder & Stoughton, 1979.

Richard Foster, *Celebration of Discipline*, Hodder & Stoughton, 1989.

Richard J. Goossen and R. Paul Stevens, *Entrepreneurial Leadership: Finding Your Calling, Making a Difference*, IVP, 2013.

Billy Graham, *Peace with God: The Secret Happiness*, Doubleday, 1953.

Mark Greene, *Fruitfulness on the Frontline: Making a Difference Where You Are*, IVP, 2014.

Os Guinness, *The Call: Finding and Fulfilling the Central Purpose of Your Life*, Word Publishing, 1998.

Charles Handy, *The Age of Unreason*, Random House, 1998.

Peter S. Heslam, 'Christianity and the Prospects for Development in the Global South', *The Oxford Handbook of Christianity and Economics* (ed. Paul Oslington), Oxford University Press, 2014, ch. 19.

Richard Higginson, *Faith, Hope and the Global Economy*, IVP, 2012.

Richard Higginson, *Questions of Business Life*, Authentic Lifestyle, 2002.

David J. Jeremy, *Capitalists and Christians: Business Leaders and the Churches in Britain 1900–1960*, Oxford University Press, 1990.

Jerry Marshall, *Travels with an Inflatable Elephant: Attempts to Make Things Happen and Not Happen*, Instant Apostle, 2013.

Anita Roddick, *Body and Soul*, Ebury Press, 1991.

John Sentamu (ed.), *On Rock or Sand? Firm Foundations for Britain's Future*, SPCK, 2015.

Robert Solomon, *Ethics and Excellence: Cooperation and Integrity in Business*, Oxford University Press, 1992.

Jeff Van Duzer, *Why Business Matters to God (And What Still Needs to be Fixed)*, IVP, 2010.

Michael Volland, *The Minister as Entrepreneur: Leading and Growing the Church in an Age of Rapid Change*, SPCK, 2015.

James Walvin, *The Quakers: Money and Morals*, John Murray,
    1997.

Max Weber, *The Protestant Ethic and the Spirit of Capitalism*,
    Routledge Classics, 2001.

Peter Webster with Shirley Jenner, *The Resilient Business:
    Embedding Christian Values in Your Company's DNA*, Jubilee
    Centre, 2016.

Christopher J. H. Wright, *The Mission of God's People: A Biblical
    Theology of the Church's Mission*, Zondervan, 2010.

Articles

Business Reporter, 'The Big Interview: Luke Johnson,
    Entrepreneur', 29 March 2016.

Richard J. Goossen, 'The Christian Entrepreneur: Worthy
    of His Calling?', *Faith in Business Quarterly* 10:3, pp. 6–11.

Andrew Henley, 'Does Religion Influence Entrepreneurial
    Behaviour?', unpublished paper.

Peter Heslam, 'Pioneers of Prosperity: Entrepreneurial Role
    Models as Sources of Hope and Inspiration', *Faith in Business
    Quarterly* 13:2, pp. 33–34.

Peter Heslam and Eric Wood, 'Belief in Enterprise: Christian
    Entrepreneurs in the Global Economy', *Faith in Business
    Quarterly* 14:4, pp. 33–34.

Peter Heslam and Eric Wood, 'Fully and Gloriously Alive:
    Virtuous Human Development', *Faith in Business Quarterly*
    17:1, pp. 33–34.

Peter Heslam and Eric Wood, 'Pride of Africa: The Rise of the
    Lion Economics', *Faith in Business Quarterly* 15:3, pp. 33–34.

Lancaster Guardian, 'Hotel Group Keeps It in the Family for
    National Award', 12 June 2016.

Lausanne Occasional Paper no. 59, *Business as Mission: A New
    Vision, A New Heart, A Renewed Call*, 2004.

Northwich Guardian, 'Family Firm Set to Create Largest Manufacturing Hub in North West', 2012.

Kina Robertshaw, 'Asking Big Questions: Life at the Mitchell Group', *Faith in Business Quarterly* 16:3, pp. 13–15.

Kina Robertshaw, 'Lawsons: A Family Business with a Difference', *Faith in Business Quarterly* 16:4, pp. 24–26.

The Guardian, 'The Entertainer: Inside the HQ of the UK's Growing Toy Empire', 28 April 2016.

Websites

http://allia.org.uk/future-business-centres
www.anglorecycling.com
www.beulahlondon.com
www.carpintree.co.uk
www.cygnet-group.org
www.davidballgroup.co.uk
www.design2market.co.uk
www.eden.co.uk/christian-books
www.handinhandgroup.co.uk
http://higham.co.uk
http://isleofman-companies.com
www.littletrove.com
www.reynoldstechnology.biz
www.schlutercoffee.co.uk
www.therooflightcompany.co.uk
http://thesaintsprojectstrust.org
www.thetoyshop.com/aboutus